LOVE,   SEX   AND

DAVID   C.   DOEL

THE   LINDSEY   PRESS
LONDON

Printed in Great Britain by
Jervis Printers
78 Stockport Road, Ashton-Under-Lyne,
Lancs Ol7 0LH

ISBN   0 85319 0569

Published by the Lindsey Press
Essex Hall,
1-6   Essex Street,
Strand,
London
WC2R 3HY

1996

L O V E , S E X A N D T H E S P I R I T:

THE CREATIVE CHALLENGE OF DEVIANCE

BY

DAVID CHARLES DOEL

8 Old Rd.,
Dukinfield,
Cheshire,
SK16 4 EN
0161 339 4476

CONTENTS
ACKNOWLEDGEMENTS
INTRODUCTION

BIBLIOGRAPHY

GLOSSARY

ACKNOWLEDGMENTS

I am most grateful to Matthew Smith and the Unitarian Information Department for their work in the production of this book and for Lindsey Press patronage.

I would like to acknowledge permission to publish passages of text from works published by the following publishers (Full details of the works referred to appear in the Bibliography and chapter notes):   Basic Books, Black Swan Books, Columbia University Press, Darton, Longman and Todd, Faber and Faber, Hogarth Press, Methuen, Penguin Books, Picador Books and Routledge.

INTRODUCTION

In the present climate of thought and feeling about sexual abuse one is wary of suggesting that, horrendous though abuse may be both at the time of abuse and in its powerfully debilitating effects over many years, it is possible for people who have been abused to work through their rage, grief and humiliation to a creative resolution of their trauma; even to a new and fruitful relationship between abused and abuser. I worked with a woman who had been sexually abused over several years during her puberty and adolescence, by her father and brother. The experience of abuse had scarred her life, filled her with shame and guilt and soured her relationships with her husband and son. But she was able to work through in therapy to the point where she was able to see how this abuse had grown out of her father's and her brother's isolation, their fear of women and deep craving for intimacy; to be able not only to understand the abuse, but to forgive it and establish fresh and creative relationships with father and brother and also her mother, whom she had hated for her covert collusion and silence.

A man I worked with, who had been raped, forcibly buggered as a youth at work, over a bench by an older, stronger man, was haunted by this memory through several years of difficult therapy - yet, as it turned out, he eventually found himself able not only to understand and forgive his abuser, but to recognise that through his engagement with the painful effects of his abuse he had gained insights, strengths and understanding that might well otherwise have eluded him. As Green and Townsend argue in their studies of sexual abuse in *Hidden Treasure*, one can grow towards the place where even the most traumatic abuse and horrific pathology may be transformed richly and creatively; discover in the words of one of their contributors how "the whole sordid mess" may be transformed into "something beautiful, a hidden treasure beyond value and price."

Clearly, the eventual creative outcome of any person's abuse is no justification whatsoever for that or any other abuse. The work of researchers such as Green and Townsend should, nonetheless, give us pause, beyond our natural indignation, to consider more closely the psychodynamic and theological implications of abuse, not only for the abused and the abuser, but also for all of us, who share the same social context out of which abuse arises.

The insight into gender issues provided by the study of sexual abuse, deviance and perversion, has been enormous. Deviancy and perversion, indeed, may be seen now not merely as an abberation from the norm, but as a covert, unconscious bid for freedom and a potentially creative challenge from which we have so much to learn about the common roots of deviance in so-called 'normal life'. Deviance offers an unexpected and unlikely theatre of experience from which we may gain startling and illuminating glimpses into forms of oppression deeply affecting the theologies, the politics, the conventions and mores of whole societies. We are able to apply insights gained from our deeper understanding of sexual deviance to deviance as difference, wherever it reveals itself as a challenge to the status quo.

The study of the reaction of communities to sexual deviancy helps us, for example, to understand the communal rejection of other styles of deviancy - the persecution and destruction of great deviants like Socrates, Jesus of Nazareth and Galileo; and the excommunication of deviants as heretics by institutions such as the church. We may see how often social and cultural change and 'progress' has come through the courageous commitment of gifted deviants - for example, the martyrs of the Reformation, the suffragettes in Britain and, recently, the struggles of Ellen Russell and Sarah Waddington, which led to changes in Texan Anti-abortion legislation.

Women, in particular, have suffered as deviants, since the mere fact of being a woman in a patriarchal world, a single sex or phallic universe (to use Lacan's phrase) has placed women inexorably in the role of deviant, even where they have conformed to the mores. No human group, indeed, has suffered more from long-established sexual conventions and gender mores than women. Feminist writers have made us all aware how men have dominated and abused women throughout recorded history. If anyone had doubted the appalling subjugation of women, the accumulated evidence is now beyond rejection. In this book I have explored the question: why should men have felt it necessary or appropriate or even desired to subjugate women and why have women so often readily colluded in it? I seek some explanation for the terror which lies behind the abuse of women down the centuries and in our own time; and of the extraordinary anxiety to hold onto conventional views of marriage and sexual relationships. I would like to understand why human beings have been so afraid of homosexuality, adultery and the change in the status of women that the penalties for those who dared offend against the mores of sex and gender have often been more severe than the penalties even for rape or murder.

Out of a fascination with the interface of psychotherapy and religion, of theology and psychodynamics, I have considered in this book the relationships between Love, Sex and the Spirit, whilst engaging with the stimulating challenge of postmodern feminist writers and their illuminating insights into sexuality, difference, deviance and perversion: for example, the intriguing psycho/theological implications of the suggestion by Luce Irigaray that the primary trauma of separation is not at the oedipal position or during weaning, but in the severing of the umbilical cord; and that in sexual intercourse the penis becomes an umbilical phallus, a tube joining two bodies, through which the partners attempt to re-enter the Mother, make a return to the Womb as Abyss - an unconscious invitation to be born again.

In the first chapter I have elaborated some of the philosophical and theological implications of the concept of the Abyss, a metaphor that has exercised (under different names, such as the Void, the Chora, the Dark Night of the Soul and Pure Absence) the imagination of thinkers as widely separated in time and space.as Plato, Heidegger, Jacques Derrida, St. John of the Cross and the Buddha. The Abyss represents the 'space' between Being and Non-Being; between having no sense of a separate identity and discovering an identity in the process of weaning; the 'space' beyond my conception of who I am.

As Beck and Beck-Gernsheim argue in *The Normal Chaos of Love*, people hold together their sense of identity through the traditions of the culture to which they belong, through universal conventions and mores marking out the roles of men and women towards each other and their community. Now that these mores have fallen away and generations have grown up in a new milieu of 'individualism', what it means to be partners or parents or members of a community, is in the melting pot and all manner of relational experiments are afoot: living together without 'benefit' of marriage, single-parent families, lesbian and gay partnerships and so on.

Our culturally derived defences against loss of identity, against regression into the Abyss are considerably weakened by this revolutionary change in our attitudes towards marriage and parenting and work and leisure. Consequently the commonest presenting symptoms in counselling now are existential or ontological problems of angst, meaninglessness, pointlessness, issues concerning personal identity; the sense of having become deviant in society, not belonging and no longer held by its mores - clearly religious issues.

People still seek meaning and fulfilment through their working/career roles, but primarily, more and more, through the love of partners and/or children. These relationships have become powerfully invested with the hope of giving life meaning, of shoring up the boundaries of our sense of identity and of providing us with personal fulfilment. The failure of such hopes - and their attendant phantasies - to secure persistent realisation in our relationships, and the deep and bitter disappointment felt by people when they do fail, is related to the accelerating rate of divorce and the disturbing increase of violence in the home.

Postmodernist thinkers have restated the ancient claim of our greatest poets, that our flight from the Abyss through conventional adherence to the received knowledge of our culture and our pursuit of personal fulfilment through the affirmation of our sense of identity in relation to the mores of our community, is doomed to failure. This position is of special significance for Unitarians - ourselves a deviant, still marginalised movement - concerned to protect individual liberty, freedom and integrity against dogmatism, social prejudice and any kind of tyranny. The assimilation of Postmodernist Feminism into our Unitarian theology is vital if we are to avoid, in the next century, appearing as a rather respectable, anacronistic form of liberal fundamentalism. We are challenged by Postmodernism into a revival in our own time of the implications of our Protesting, Nonconforming and Radical Dissenting heritage.

Flights into the 'up' world rob us not only of the possibility of discovering our own unique potentiality - the treasures that lie in the 'down' world of the Abyss - but also deprive us of what we most desire, that is Love. For Love cannot be sustained in living out unassimilated, and therefore infantile phantasies, in relation to the overt world. Love is, ironically, the Face revealed in the Abyss as we struggle together in pain and in joy along the dark, regressive path of Deconstruction, through which we may discover, so the postmodernists promise, *jouissance* - or, as Freud (and Augustine) had it, Love, Energy and Freedom from Fear: "Where id was, there shall ego be. It is reclamation work, like the draining of the Zuyder Zee."

Readers unversed in postmodernist philosophy or theology will find the first chapter difficult and should begin reading at chapter two (a revision and development of a chapter from my *Out of Clouds and Darkness*), coming back to chapter one after reading chapters two to six. A glossary is appended after the Bibliography.

CHAPTER ONE

THE ABYSS

The word for abyss - Abgrund - originally means the soil and ground towards which, because it is undermost, a thing tends downward ... But in what follows, we shall think of the ab- as the complete absence of the ground. The age for which the ground fails to come, hangs in the abyss.

Martin Heidegger
(What Are Poets For?)

The present moment is always full of infinite treasure, it contains far more than you have the capacity to hold. Faith is the measure; what you find in the present moment will be according to the measure of your faith. Love also is the measure: the more your heart loves, the more it desires, and the more it desires the more it finds ... The divine will is an abyss, the opening of which is the present moment. Plunge into this abyss and you will find it ever deeper than your desires.

Jean-Pierre de Caussade
(Self-Abandonment to Divine Providence)

Where the swirling waves gather there is an abyss; where the still waters gather there is an abyss; where the running waters gather there is an abyss. The abyss has nine names ... Just now I appeared to him as Not Yet Emerged From My Source. I came at him empty, wriggling and turning, not knowing anything about 'who' or 'what', now dipping and bending, now flowing in waves - that's why he ran away.

Chuang Tzu

Fit For Emperors And Kings

Only pure absence - not the absence of this or that, but the absence of everything in which all presence is announced - can inspire, in other words can work, and then make one work.

Jacques Derrida
Force and Signification

A dream commonly reported in psychotherapeutic sessions is of falling from one knows not where down to one knows not where. The dreamer is filled with dread as if the fall were a descent into a vast, empty abyss - a nothingness more absent of presence than the nothingness of outer space. The dreamer makes a colossal effort to brake the fall and awakes in a powerful and painful physical spasm, sweating with fear, tense in every muscle of the body.

The dream offers an astonishing, highly creative possibility for the dreaming Ego, of falling out of its familiar constructed sense of identity into the experience of soullessness or self-loss; the loss of self which preludes the discovery of Self; the return to Primary Narcissism. The Ego, however, is convinced that beyond the boundaries of its constructed, conditioned sense of identity lies only madness or death. Its terror deprives it of any fragile faith that outside the boundaries of self, in the abyss, lies great treasure, anything so positively astonishing as 'the Commonwealth of God' (degenderised alternative to 'Kingdom of God'). Chaos (the primordial formless void) and confusion (the vertigo of freedom, the threat of disturbed foundations) are intolerable to the Ego as it views the world from the narrow prison of its own climes. Indeed, the more fragile the prison walls, the less tolerance the Ego has for deviance, for difference; desperately the Ego shores up the bricks of dogmatism and the bars of cultural mores. And nowhere does it feel more vulnerable than where the serpent swings its tail - in the volatile cosmos of sex, gender and love.

"Now we see as in a mirror *(esoptron),* darkly," says Saint Paul in his Hymn to Love, (I.Cor. XIII) "but then face to face. Now we know in part, but then shall we know even as now we are known." *Esoptron* was a looking glass made of polished metal. The Latin for mirror was *speculum* - to look at, to speculate. Our word 'mirror' comes from neither of these words, but from the Latin *mirare*, meaning to wonder or to admire, to look at. The words 'mirage' and 'miracle' come from the same root - and in the background is a Sanskrit root, *'meera'*, meaning the Divine Mother, not unrelated to 'Mary' (from Hebrew 'Miriam' - meaning, perhaps, 'the wished for child', or *'Marat'*, 'burnished and polished'). Now there's a rich and pregnant etymology if ever there was one!

Somewhere during the process of weaning - in the move from non-differentiation to differentiation of self, from being a 'non-self' to becoming a 'self', from being a 'no-one' to becoming a 'someone' - human beings learn to use the world as a mirror and accept the mirage of the mirrored world as reality. Through the eyes of the (Divine) Mother (of whatever sex) the infant sees reflected who she is and falls in love, like Narcissus, with that image. So we fall in love with ourselves, the 'self' which emerges from the love we bear for the (Divine) Mother. Spiritual languor eventually comes upon us, soon or late, as it came upon Narcissus, since we are now in love (*cupiditas* in Augustine) with a pale reflection of our true self and an impossible chasm has appeared between who we are and who we have become.

THE MIRROR STAGE

At an international congress of Psychoanalysis in 1936 Lacan introduced his concept of the Mirror Stage, elaborated in a later paper to the Congress in 1949 (with reference to Plato's allegory of The Cave), as "formative of the function of the I" (1). Lacan referred to Kohler's discovery that a child, at the age when s/he is outdone by the chimpanzee in 'instrumental intelligence', can already recognise her own image in a mirror. This act, far from exhausting itself, as in the case of the chimpanzee, once the image is found empty, becomes for the child a game "in which he experiences in play the relation between the movements assumed in the image and the reflected environment, and between this virtual complex and the reality it duplicates" - i.e. the child's own body, and the persons and things around her.

According to Lacan the recognition of one's corporeal self through our mirrored image distinguishes the human from the animal. The mere sight "of the total form of the human body", Lacan insists, "gives the subject an imaginary mastery of his/her body," prematurely in relation to the real mastery. The mirror stage inaugurates a "concept of self" through the "identification with the image as semblance". Lorraine Gauthier, in *The Hysterical Male* (2), elaborating Lacan's concept of the mirror stage, declares that between the self constructed upon the mirror images received primarily through my parents (or other caretaking figures), i.e. my conditioned identity, and the self which may, as it were, stand apart and 'view' that mirrored self as a construct, lies "a gap".

There is a gap, an abyss, at the heart of my sense of identity. Only as I recognise the gap between my self as conscious Ego (i.e. prereflective consciousness) and my self as construct, a mirrored self - an Ego system or identity - can I see that there is a self as Other; to say the least, that there is my self as potentia - whom I could have been if I had not been seduced into these particular identifications.

I am conscious of myself as having a certain identity, however fluid that sense of identity (my Ego system). But my consciousness is not to be identified with that identity (Ego system) since, in existentialist terms, my pre-reflective consciousness precedes the cogito. In other words: 'I am aware of thinking' is primary to "I am thinking'. I am not my thought processes, so much as my awareness, consciousness of them. Just as I may identify with a character on the television screen and, in some sense, 'become' that character through 'identification', nonetheless my awareness of the character, my consciousness of the movements on the screen, are primary to the identification with that character. When I 'come to myself' and stand apart to switch off the set, I become aware of myself as conscious observer of what is now a blank screen. I can be conscious - aware - of nothing and self-reflectively aware that I am aware of nothing; i.e. 'no thing', even when that no-thing reveals itself as a pleroma, bursting with Love. Like Jacob Boehme I may find when words have fallen away, and I am in the beyond of language, an ecstasy arise of such intensity that, when I am myself again within the realm of language, I cannot find words to describe it.

The abyss represents the emptiness of not-knowing who I am, when I allow my identification with this or that to slip away; when I fall out of my habitual sense of self (Ego system). Inasmuch as I become absent to my self, I am able to discover myself; free from the containing restrictions of the Ego system, I may now discover areas of self hitherto ignored or unknown (i.e. unconscious). Those who lose their selves, may find them, as Jesus said. By regressing beyond my self, to the point where I was not a self-reflective, thinking self; by returning, as it were, to the womb, I may be born again. It is in this way I may gain access to the wealth in the abyss. Just as the poet by his or her absence, says Derrida (3), "allows language free access to its full range of possibility", so by our absence the full range of our human possibility becomes accessible - in the Ego-less state God may speak, be revealed. Out of the abyss, in the space made available by the self-emptied Ego, the Other may arise.

Nicodemus could not understand what depth psychologists take for granted, that I may 'return to the womb' and be 'reborn'(4). Jesus said that unless one was born both of the water (uterine?) and the spirit, one could not enter the Commonwealth of God. Nicodemus does not see his 'self' as a construct standing in the way of his 'Self'. The possibility of losing one's 'self' is beyond his imagination. For Nicodemus the world of the senses, the mirage of the real, and his imaginitive relationship with that world and its symbols and signs has become total reality. Jesus, by contrast, is clearly aware of a deep mystery at the heart of his being, a mystery which overtakes and possesses all poets in their relationship with the Muse: "The Spirit bloweth where it listeth and no-one knows where it comes from or where it goes." Is there not great irony in the incredulity of Jesus: "Are you a leader of Israel and do not understand these things?"

After all, Nicodemus would have celebrated the Passover every Spring. Interpreted through the allegorical method, in use amongst the pharisees of his time, the myth of the Passover expresses the movement of the soul from Bondage, through a Wilderness into a Promised Land. Fleeing the familiar, though degrading and now dangerously hostile, Land of Bondage, where they have been reared and which they have called their home, the people reluctantly follow the call of God across a River, whose waters will swallow up anything hindering their escape; into a Wilderness, where they wander as lost children, fed by resources beyond their own control; to a land, where their Guru may not take them, representing their true home and destiny.

The Hebrew for 'Passover', *Pesah*, was translated into the Septuagint and the New Testament with the Greek word *Pasca*, related, controversially, to the verb *Pasco*, originally meaning to suffer, to be acted upon, or ill-treated. This etymology, however inaccurate, seemed to illuminate the later use of the word 'Passion' to describe the sufferings of Christ on the Cross - as the Paschal Lamb, a scapegoat for the ills of the world. The word 'Passion' is, in fact, from the Latin *Passio* and renders the Greek *Pathos*. The Tomb, where the body of Jesus is laid, is a symbolical Abyss or Wilderness, through which Jesus 'passes over' to emerge renewed in the Resurrection - interpreted by the Gnostics as a symbol of the transformation of consciousness (5).

Crucifixion, Tomb and Resurrection represent the fate of the one who defies the Ruling Powers-That-Be within the psyche, challenging their mores, deconstructing until all margins come to the centre and a crisis of identity, a 'self-death', plunges the soul into the Abyss or Wilderness, from which it may arise transformed by a new relationship with its own depths - a condition described by the Christians as being 'filled with the Holy Spirit.' The myth of the Crucifixion, Tomb and Resurrection give power to the saying of Jesus that only those who lost their 'self' *(Psyche)*, by denying their 'self' and taking up their Cross, would find their 'self' (6). (The Greek *arneomai*, translated 'to deny' meant, rather, in this mode of Middle Voice, something like 'destroy for one's own benefit'.)

THE UNION OF NOTHING WITH NOTHING

The Tomb is an Abyss, an Emptiness, a Dark Night, a Cloud of Unknowing. "For when I say darkness," wrote the author of the Cloud of Unknowing (7), "I mean a lack of knowing ... so put a cloud of forgetting beneath thee, betwixt thee and all the creatures that ever be made." In his postscript to The Cloud of Unknowing, the seventeenth century director of the spiritual life, Father Augustine Baker, writes of the mystic union as a union of nothing with nothing; an application of the soul, "being for the time rid of all images - to God." Here, the soul discerns "neither time nor place nor image, but a certain vacuity or emptiness, both as in regard of herself as of all other things."

To grasp the operation of creative imagination, writes Derrida in *Force and Signification* (8), "one must turn oneself toward the invisible interior of poetic freedom. One must be separated from oneself in order to be reunited with the blind origin of the work in its darkness." In *Violence and Metaphysics* (9), Derrida expounds the 'messianic eschatology' of Emmanuel Levinas, declaiming that in the 'heart of the desert', in the 'growing wasteland', the thought of Levinas "makes us dream of an inconceivable process of dismantling and dispossession". Messianic eschatology:

> is but a question of designating a space or a hollow within naked
> experience where this eschatology can be understood and where it must
> resonate. This hollow space is not an opening among others. It is
> opening itself, the opening of opening, that which can be enclosed
> within no category or totality, that is, everything within experience which
> can no longer be described by traditional concepts, and which resists
> every philosopheme.

The Abyss opens into a plenum void. It is the doorway into the Commonwealth of God, the gate into Nirvana; yet the possibility of so much as touching the hem of the skirt of that dark mystery terrifies us beyond anything in creation. Contemplatives the world over - amongst the Sufis of Islam, in Buddhism, Judaism, Hinduism and Christianity - speak of the great benefits arising in this dark void of emptiness and unknowing. For Love is the Face we see in the Abyss. Love is prior to Being, as the French postmodernist philosopher and theologian, Jean-Luc Marion (10), assures us. God is not Being, essentially, primordially, but Love. Being arises out of Love. Love gives Being to Non-Being.

What sort of paradox is this that Love, which we all desire, terrifies the very wits out of us until we flee in haste, as from the Hound of Heaven, through the labyrinthine ways of our own minds, hiding in the midst of tears? After all, we have it on no less an authority than St. John of the Cross (11) that: "The greater is the darkness wherein the soul journeys and the more completely is it voided of its natural operations, the greater is its security."

Buddist teachers say there are two sides to the Void - a dark side and a light side. We approach the Void through the darkness of our own ignorance and self-centredness, imprisoned by desire. Only when we have learned to rely on nothing at all do we discover the serenity and bliss of the light side of the Void. The darkness gives us pause. An unbelievable horror, from which we are in flight, over which we have constructed our sense of identity, threatens to become accessible to us. We hesitate to surrender the defences built against an experience, or set of experiences, so painful, so harrowing, it seems we would die rather than make our Primal Scream.

REGRESSION TO THE FEMININE

The psychoanalyst, Harry Guntrip, in *Schizoid Phenomena, Object Relations and the Self* (12), describes how, observing the regressive programme in his clients, he became impressed with their narrowing concentration - through the Oedipal Position, the Depressive and Schizoidal Positions - on one unvarying central feature of their inner experience: "Somewhere deep within them they come upon the feeling of being absolutely and utterly alone, or of being about to fall into such a condition." His clinical experience suggested that of all the ultimate terrors, the last and worst was the feeling of being "a psyche in a vacuum", out of all touch, out of all relationship, empty of all experience, "and so to speak collapsing in on itself, lost in a sense of complete unreality, and unable to be an 'ego'".

One of my own clients, regressing deeply, said he felt he had made touch with his infant self and as he intuited his way into that infant's existenz it was as if he had been abandoned by his parents on an empty ice flow in the Arctic ocean and had just watched their ship disappear over the dark horizon.

Guntrip declared the conscious Ego was the Ego of separation, of 'doing', of acting and being acted on, and in that sense was "the location of the male element in personality." Its strength derived, however, "from the deepest unconscious core of the self" that had never lost "the feeling of 'being-at-one-with' the maternal source of its life" and the security of the womb. Regression thus became the fruit of the deconstructive analysis of the 'self', leading through the classical 'positions' to what Guntrip called the 'safe inside experience', which might well mean 'a return to the womb' and 'a being born again' into a new, vital relationship with the archetypal feminine gender (the anima). Engagement with the archetypal gender figures, anima and animus, deconstructs and reinforms the socially conditioned definitions of gender imposed on us from infancy.

Julia Kristeva (13), a Postmodernist Feminist Philosopher and Psychoanalyst, has elaborated a concept of 'maternal space', deriving from a passage in Heidegger, where he revealed his interest in the notion of *chora* in Plato: "Between beings and Being there prevails the *chorismos; chora* is the locus, the site, the place". Heidegger was fascinated by this highly ambiguous spatial category found in pre-Socratic thought as well as in Plato - a space, a clearing, he wrote, an open centre which is "not surrounded by what is"; rather, the centre "itself encircles all that is, like the Nothing we scarcely know." This clearing "in which beings stand is in itself at the same time concealment"(14).

Kristeva conceives the *chora* as a concept of space which is gendered Feminine - a Maternal place. The great mystics, she believes, did indeed occupy "this negative and liminal place of the Mother" and in *Tales of Love* she asserts that "Freedom with respect to the Maternal territory then becomes the pedestal upon which Love of God is erected". This Love is revealed through "the dissolution of subjectivity, of the boundaries between self and other", residing in the gap between death and eternity, since as 'amour' it can incoporate death as 'a-mort'or 'undeath'. Kristeva suggests the figure of the Virgin Mary, whose bodily Assumption is emphasised in her *Stabat Mater* (15), captures the mystical notion of a mode of being which is mysteriously empty, but whose emptiness is precisely the context in which a new kind of Love may appear.

Regression to infancy, to the experience of the womb, involves an engagement with both aspects of the Divine Mother - the castrating Mother of the weaning period and the blissful Mother of the womb. The separating, differentiating of the Ego, of the sense of my separate identity, of my need to act and mark out, demarcate and split the psyche, produces a masculinisation of the Ego-system and an initiation into a world where the Divine Father rules, where masculine values, unbalanced in terror against feminine values, have become Patriarchal macho values. The name of the game now is alienation - the Separated condition of Sin.

LANGUAGE AND SEPARATION

The most effective weapon in the Father's macho world, the tool of Separation, becomes language. "Nothing exists outside the text," says Derrida; language thinks us.   How to escape the words, there's the rub!   Every meditator or would-be-contemplative knows   s/he cannot avoid the words. We think we think our thoughts, but any serious attempt to still the mind reveals how inexorably thoughts think us. Language stands between our selves and who we truly are; it plays restless sentinel at the busy threshold of consciousness, lest we fall into the Abyss, towards the Maternal Womb, the dark inside world of the Eternal Feminine.

Contemplatives teach all manner of techniques for stilling the mind, for breaking the stranglehold of language: monitoring the breath as it courses in and out of the nostrils; chanting mantras (*man* to think and *tr* to cross over - a crossing over through thought), - *AUM, kyrie eleison*; concentrating on the flickering flame of a candle; the heat in the palms of the hands.   But how very difficult it is to maintain even a single recollected image, let alone reach the imageless state of *Samadhi*, enter *Nibbana*, where consciousness is emptied of all images, and loses even the distinctions of time and space.

It is not that language is evil *per se*. Hindu philsophers, who emphasise the Veda as oral and down play the written text, believe   the spoken sacred word reveals divine truth and has power to transform consciousness.   There are, however, words, mere words, and sacred words. There is language which imprisons and language which sets free.   But at the core of human nature, that which was there from the beginning, is nothing that can be named.   All words, sacred and profane, must finally be set aside if Brahman is to speak to the soul.

Indian thinkers have seen philosophy as a pathway to liberation or release and not merely as theoretical knowledge.   Philosophy must, somehow, lead to transformation in our lives - have practical application. This is true, also, of Derrida and his method of deconstruction. It is designed to transform our understanding and perception of ourselves and our world; the method questions all polarisations; it recognises how our use of language unconsciously solidifies our prejudices and sustains the dominion of the macho rule - the prison-house of the mores as received   knowledge.   Out of terror of the Abyss we hold, however unwittingly, to these values and gain strength to withstand our own Core, it seems, in the solidarity craved by modernism: in the dogmatism of demarcation, measurement and discrimination. Tearing its intellectual nails as it scampers from the Pit, the Ego of the modernist enterprise desires desperately to believe we may hold (if not now then in some not too distant future, thanks to the Empiricial Method and the Verification Principles) the complete truth about our world - that the shadows are not only real, but also Reality.

Difference is hardly tolerable in that modernist macho world. People who are different, who deviate, and concepts expressing difference, especially the Feminine, threaten its closed and inter-locked systems of language, where words must lack ambiguity; and bring us trembling to the untenable possibility of the terror of unknowing, of confusion and chaos. The horror of regression, of descent, towards the dark side of the void so painfully closed to us through educational conditioning at home, school and play assures we cling to language as it thinks us. Deconstruction attempts to drive a wedge between one word and another, to create a fulcrum that might move our spiritual world. We are asked, especially, for example, to look at the hierarchical complementary pairs embedded in conventional, already polarised, modernist use of language - like Right and Wrong; God and the Devil; Male and Female; King and Queen; Active and Passive, Strong and Soft; Good and Evil; Heterosexual and Homosexual; Presence and Absence - and so on.

Derrida has a Jewish heritage and is much influenced by Rabbinic thought. Whereas Greek thought provided the main source of Western logocentric metaphysics, Derrida's sympathies are with (what he perceives as) an opposing stream of Western thought deriving from Judaism, in which metaphor is seen as logical statement (quite contrary to Aristotle's logic of the excluded middle - things either are or are not!) and where diversity, multiple meaning and interrelationship are emphasised.

Harold Coward has written an illuminating account of the parallels between Derrida's philosophy and that of Buddhist and Hindu thinkers (16). The fluidity and creative ambiguity in Derrida's use of language is, Coward believes, paralleled in Eastern philosophy, where language is also seen both as revealing of the mysteries of the Void and also, at the same time, as a barrier against our own depths, obfuscating our vision until we are trapped in the world of illusion (*maya*).

In the Vedas speech is equated with Brahman. One Aranyaka actually states "the whole of Speech is Brahman".   Speech is seen as the support of all creation. Prajapati (Author of Creation) and Speech are viewed as male and female copulating to create the world. The Brahmanical tradition takes language itself as of Divine origin, as Spirit descending and embodying itself in phenomena, assuming various guises and disclosing its real nature to the sensitive soul (17).

The AUM, the so-called 'seed sound', incorporates all three levels of consciousness - waking, dreaming and deep sleep - and reaches out to the transcendent where sound itself comes to an end. Lost in appearances - *samsara*

- we fail to penetrate to the deeper reality that the language of scripture would reveal; i.e. point to, signify. For Buddhists, too - although often appearing to reject this tradition of the spiritual value of 'sacred' language - spiritual release requires an escape from our ordinary encapsulation in language and its distorting *avidya* of subject-object duality (18).

Derrida applauds statements by Hindu philosophers that, although speaking and sound are primary, it is a category mistake to identify the physical sound as the word. The essence of language is not speech, says Derrida, but writing. Language is always there, from the beginning, emerging from the beginningless state he calls the Arche (like God, before Being!). Derrida does not want to trace the origin of language in either direction - inward to the Divine Logos, Speech from the beyond of the Abyss; or outward to the 'conventional sign'. So that 'writing' is being used in a special sense characterising both inner and outer worlds. Even DNA is a form of language, says Derrida (tongue in cheek?). Writing is, thus, before speech.

THE ARCHE TRACE

Derrida's talk of trace writing or arche-writing coresponds somewhat, it seems, to the Jungian and Augustinian notions of archetype - there from the beginning or beginningless. But, for Derrida, the Arche is an imprint without an imprinter; a 'Being' that arises out of 'Non-Being'. Marion (see above), similarly describes Being as that which arises out of Non-Being - a Non-Being, however, which is Love (*Agape*). Clearly for Derrida and negative (apophatic) theologians of all traditions there has to be a 'passing over' between Non-Being and Being; betweeen not existing and existing; between being nothing and being something; between atemporality and temporality; between being animal and being 'rational animal'. Despite his assertions against the title of negative theologian Derrida's writing is sometimes astonishingly reminiscent of the Johannine prologue: "In the beginning was the Word, and the Word was with God, and the Word was God. He was in the beginning with God, all things were made through him, and without the Word was not anything made that was made."

There is no source or ground of language outside of language itself. Nothing is outside the text. But Derrida's use of the term 'arche' is, it seems, his way of circumventing the perpetual metaphysical, ontological puzzle (in physics, cosmology, depth psychology and philosophy) of how anything may arise out of nothing; Being out of Non-Being; Finite out of Infinite; presence out of absence.

Derrida accuses western philosophers (and sometimes Eastern philosophy as well) of answering the question of the nature of Being in terms of presence; philosophers, he says, posit a Being, such as God or Brahman, Whose Presence gives - from the Beyond of the Abyss - meaning to language (imprinting the Logos in creation). No matter how strongly such 'logocentrism' (as Derrida calls it - 'the belief in the self-presentation of meaning') might describe God as essentially transcendent or unknowable, God remains a convenient axiom, a kind of final Solution, or ultimate full stop, with which all the profoundest questions of ontology may be silenced; and a belief in the essential unity of all things be preserved. For Derrida the basis of Being and of Language is not unity, but difference. Arche-writing is nothing but dynamic, expressive differance - to differ and to defer. Although arche-writing cannot be said to 'exist', its possibility is anterior to all expressions (signified, signifier, content-expression, etc.). Differance, not unity, actually permits the articulation of speech and writing and founds the metaphysical opposition between signifier and signified. Differance is therefore, he says, the formation of form and the being imprinted of the imprint; it marks the passage from non-being to being. Language is a dynamic becoming that is itself the very stuff of our experience of reality.

Language has a life of its own. Poets allow language to overwhelm them and step out of the way, self-emptied of the restrictive, hypnotic mirage of constructed and conditioned language, so that language, rid of stereotypical and polarised inhibition, can express itself freely. It appears as if, for Derrida, the experience of Self is the unobstructed experience of arche-writing manifested in the temporal dynamic of language. Obstacles to this experience are identified as the incorrect understanding and use of language forms and the 'ego-knots'such impure useage produces.

Derrida uses the word 'Sign' to refer to the whole, signified to refer to the abstract concept and signifier to refer to the spoken and heard sound image. The sign, or linguistic whole, is differentiated by spacing (on the page) and by interval or pause (in speech). The actualising of this inherent force (telos!) for differentiation enables language to function; but is, at the self same time, the defining limit of language - since a sign cannot be produced within the plenitude of absolute Presence. Therefore, there can be no absolute truth or complete meaning expressed through language. How close we are now to the words of Lao Tzu: "The Tao that can be spoken is not the eternal Tao"; or of Hegel: "When speaks the soul, alas, the soul no longer speaks." (19)

Ironically, however, where Lao Tzu and Hegel are grieving the inability of language to reveal the Tao, Derrida (like the Hindu philosopher, Bhartrhari) is emphasising the positive contribution of language - it is precisely in the dynamic tension of the manifestation of the sign that truth may be found. Here there is, certainly, no cynicism concerning language, but, on the contrary, truth is seen as contained in the very dynamics of language itself.

In Hindu thought the Veda is the outward linguistic form of the dynamic self-manifesting act of the Word-Principle itself, as the Bible was the Word of God for Christian theologians. Derrida, similarly, conceives of the Word, the arche-writing, as coming upon us like the Hebrew Yahweh, but emphasises its challenge to action. It is essentially dynamic and desiring of change. Language is thus a means of self or spiritual realisation. Derrida refers to this proposal, however, as non-theistic. The theological, he says, is a determined moment in the total movement of the trace; theology is a historically second dissimulation of the trace. It is the direct experience of the dynamic process of becoming, not as a process of static reflection or metaphysical opposition, that would, says Derrida, make for the realisation of the spiritual whole; requiring deconstruction of illusions of permanence, of stasis or presence. Deconstruction is, thus, the very means of becoming self-aware - of self-realisation.

Like Sankara, for Derrida philosophy is the philosophy of language. "Il n'y a pas d' hors-texte!" For Sankara, however, there is, of course, a Real world that exists over and above language - Brahman, a world of Silence. But is not this the world of the Arche-trace? Though Derrida stresses the need for silence he does not end up in a silence totally transcending language. In his reading of Jabes (20), for example, Derrida describes God's silence as that which both speaks and stifles itself so that we may have freedom to hear and be heard. Language, even that of the Book, ends in silence - not in the silence of pure bliss, but in a silence filled with the tension of divine interrogation. God must hide to protect our freedom and reveals Presence through Absence - so that God is always a missing God, though leaving 'divine imperatives' like footprints on the landscape of the soul, already dissolving in the snow.

The Arche-trace thus has, after all, teleological implications. It contains within itself all the possibilities of manifestation as the primordial difference. This difference is the inherent teleological force within us that leads to Self-manifestation. Language speaks and writes us, impelling us into action. The emphasis in Logocentrism on Presence, he feels, seeks to absorb all differences into identity. But God is, irrevocably, irretrievably always Other - a Thou in relation to an I. No-one may see God and live. As Presence God is an Absence.

Despite his disclaimers, it seems Derrida skirts continually the fringe of apophatic, so-called negative theology and whilst Love is a concept conspicuous by its absence in the main body of his writing, he does, nonetheless, hold out the promise, beyond deconstruction, of the untranslatable *Jouissance.*

Poetry, Derrida concludes, is special because it allows us to reach the pure possibility of language. The revelatory power of poetry, he says, is the access to free speech. The 'absence' of the poet allows language free access - this is the nature of inspiration. Poetry is the anguish of *Ruach* (wind or spirit) experiencing solitude:

One must have a mind of winter
To regard the frost and the boughs
Of the pine-trees crusted with snow;

And have been cold a long time
To behold the junipers shagged with ice,
The spruces rough in the distant glitter

Of the January sun; and not to think
Of any miseries in the sound of the wind,
In the sound of a few leaves,

Which is the sound of the land
Full of the same wind
That is blowing in the same bare place

For the listener, who listens in the snow,
And, nothing himself, beholds
Nothing that is not there and the nothing that is. (21)

COLERIDGE AND LOGOCENTRICITY

No poet or philosopher was more logocentric or logosophic than Coleridge, yet there are more links between his philosophy and Postmodernism than might strike one at first glance. Like the Postmodernists, for example, he continually reassessed his own thought against the principles of distinction-in-unity, of interpersonal relations, and of dynamic polarities as methodological tools. His system involved paradox and polarity and a continuous conversation between Greek, Christian and Jewish thought. The Logos as Word, Reason, 'Alterity',

Form, combined in Coleridge with Sophia, the Spirit of love and energy, the dynamic principle of organic unity.

Like the Postmodernists Coleridge was also deeply interested in the relationship between language and our interpretation of the overt world. For example (22), Coleridge believed the veracity of words and language, and their correspondence with reality, are inseparably connected with religion and morality. His interest in Greek and Hebrew thought focused on the analogy drawn in these traditions between the divine Word (*logos* amongst the Greeks and *memra* in the Jewish tradition) and human language and speech. Words may bring to consciousness the truth already implanted by the Logos. Language is formative of consciousness, he declares; it is the process, and not only the product, of thought. The name of God given in the Old Testament (Ex. 3, 14) as 'I AM THAT I AM' was, Coleridge believed, a representation of ultimate reality in which language, and therefore philosophy, ought to be grounded. Language had been corrupted, suffered a Fall, and its misuse led to false convictions, philosophical and moral degeneration. Yet language (after Augustine) was also 'redemptive' and could be 'restored', and with it our human reason and relationships.

Kant had concluded that 'all our knowledge of God is merely symbolic', but Coleridge, along with Schelling and Goethe, would have seen the word 'merely' as a mistake. Coleridge believed the symbol, unlike the allegory which points to a unity of appearance and ideality, is "an inward unity of the objective reality of the universal idea and the subjective apperception of that reality expressed in a particular form (23)." Revelation involved the encounter of persons or personas; the Logos revealed God as both loving and willing; source and mediator of both Life and Love.

Scholastic theologians distinguished between God '*in esse*', in essential nature, and God '*per speciem*', in image form. God cannot be known in essential, transcendent Nature, they claimed, but only in image form, as revealed in dream or vision. In the space, the gap, the abyss of nothingness God would be revealed as Love. In the ecstasy of self-deconstruction or self-absence God would 'appear', per speciem, as presence. The 'appearing' God is the Logos. The God revealed in the Abyss is the Second Persona of the Trinity, the Logos or the Christ/a. The creative force or revelationary, restorative power flowing from the Abyss towards the realisation of the Potentia in the Logos or Christ/a is the Holy Spirit, the Third Persona of the Trinity. The Christ/a proceeds from God as a manifestation of divine Truth, while the Holy Spirit proceeds from God and the Christ/a as a manifestation of divine Love (Agape, Logos and Eros). The Love between God and the Christ/a is nothing less than a coequal, Third Person (the creative Third alive in each of us) . Three Personas, or aspects of God - three acting masks of God - behind which lies an essential unity, essentially unknown and unknowable.

The difference between Coleridge and the Unitarians whom he left for 'orthodoxy' was that Coleridge eventually maintained a so-called 'orthodox' (i.e. Athanasian) Trinitarian claim that Jesus of Nazareth was God incarnate in a unique and special way; whereas the Unitarian position was that best summed by James Martineau (a late contemporary of Coleridge): that the incarnation was true not of Jesus exclusively, but of all women and men universally. The 'deviant' Unitarians, still excluded from the Institute of the British Council of Churches for their heresy (24), objected to the unique identification of the man Jesus with the Second Person (i.e. the Christ or Logos). For them Jesus was a great religious poet in whom the Logos found a special home, representing the ideal union of God and humanity, of Logos and the human Reason, but the difference was one of quality or degree and not of kind; in the same way that the musical gifts of Mozart or the artistic gifts of Picasso separate them out from the rest of humanity by quality and degree and not by kind. The music flows into Mozart as a gift, he is filled by it, as Jesus is filled by his poetry, as Picasso is filled "with the sudden visions" which forced themselves upon him, so that painting was like throwing himself "into space". How else should we understand expressions such as "filled with the Holy Spirit"? Clearly, music and painting are also 'languages', through which the Eternal Word may find expression - cross the space between infinite and finite; between Non-Being and Being.

THE TRINITY

The Vedanta of India also engages a concept of incarnation, the theory of Avatara, within a doctrine of the Trinity - (not, of course, a Trinity according to Athanasius, Eusebius, Nestorius, Arius, Origen or whoever, but) the Trinity of Brahma, Vishnu and Shiva. Krishna, the human embodiment of Vishnu, the Second Person of the Trinity, who apears to Arjuna in the Bhagavadgita, is an Avatarana. Rhadakrishnan (25), discussing the Hindu Trinity in his commentary on the Gita, wrote that God "with His creative ideas" (Logoi) is Brahma. God Who pours out Love is Vishnu, perpetually at work saving the world. And, he wrote:

> When the conceptual becomes the cosmic and when heaven is established on earth, we have the fulfilment represented by Shiva.

God, he says, is at the same time wisdom, love and perfection. The three functions, personas, cannot be torn apart. Brahma, Vishnu and Shiva were fundamentally one, Brahman, though conceived as three persons. Yoga was the technique through which the Jivatmen (surface self) came to a knowledge of its union with the Paramatmen (deep unconscious, potential Self) and with Brahman (that Non-Being, Pure Consciousness, which is the Ground and Root of all Being).

It is, indeed, important that any theological position shall find an acceptable way of interpreting or deconstructing the theology of the Trinity, since the existential issues raised by the doctrine are of central concern to all the great religions of the world. What is human nature, what is the nature of God; how the transcendence of God, the Beyond of God, interacts with our universe as immanence; and the stature of our greatest religious teachers are basic questions which tax the intellect and imagination of all earnest seekers after truth in whatever religious tradition they may find themselves.

At Zurich in 1948 Jung published his revised paper on *A Psychological Approach to the Doctrine of the Trinity (26),* pointing out how the Trinity appeared in various forms in all the great religions of the world and also in the ancient religions of Egypt and Greece. He quarrelled with the doctrine as a core model for the psyche as it did not include the Fourth, the principle of Evil. A quaternity, he believed, was a more satisfactory symbol of wholeness and the unity of life. (Coleridge, incidentally, also preferred a quaternity to the notion of triunity (27), believing the tetractys, deriving from the sacred numbers and letters of the Hebrew name of God, a more satisfactory symbol and a more useful theological concept than the Trinity. The tetractys "symbolised universal ideal reality, expressing causative, dynamic relation, form, and distinction-in-unity.")

The members of the Trinity were, for Jung, archetypes of the Mother/Father (Non-Being Love as the Ground of Being), the Child (psychobiological potential - the Christ/Logos, Love emerging beyond the Gap; Being out of Non-Being) and the creative, teleological, integrative power in the psyche flowing from our potential (Eros/Holy Spirit). The Christ was an archetype of the Self. This archchetype constellated in Jesus (as it did in the Buddha in the East), who thus realised the idea of the Self, described by Jung as "the psychic totality of the individual". The goal of the individuation process (by which we realise our unique individual potentiality) was the union of the Ego (self with a small 's') with this unconscious Self. The goal of psychological as well as biological development was Self-realisation. But since we knew our own self only as an Ego, he wrote, and the Self, as a totality, was indescribable and indistinguishable from a God-image, Self-realisation in religious language amounted to God's incarnation (28).

This was expressed, Jung believed, in Christian theology by the declaration of Christ as the Child of God. The ordinary, surface self or Ego, becomes burdened on the religious quest, with the fate of losing itself in the greater dimension of the Christ image in the soul and being robbed, thereby, of the delusion of freedom of will and separateness. This 'loss of self', this surrender to the Christ or God/Self within, was an heroic and often tragic task - the most difficult of all, involving a passion of the Ego (as the Gnostics had declared).

The life of Jesus had become a paradigm for the spiritual journey everyone must take towards the realisation of that Christ/a-like potentiality innately present in us all. The Trinity thus becomes a psychological model of the basic structure and dynamics of the psyche, providing a conceptual base from which to elaborate our understanding of that journey; as well as a theological model of the Nature of God.

The Trinity embodies in a single model, extraordinarily profound and complex philosophical, psychological and theological ideas. There is God, Love Beyond Being, Pure Consciousness, becoming Self-reflective through the Logos or Christ/a in Creation (crossing the Abyss); and there is the creative, restoring power generated by that Logos or Christ/a at work in Creation. We may co-operate with that restoring power as it operates in the depths of our minds, drawing us towards the Abyss, towards 'what we have it in us to become'; or we may stand divided, split against it; which is the condition theologians have understood as Alienation, Evil or Sin. The doctrine of the Trinity attempts to express the mystery of the relationship between the Eternal and the Temporal, between God and humanity; it provides a theoretical base from which to approach the highly intuitive, positively mystical experience of human beings - the problems raised, for example, by ecstasy and possession.

It is perfectly possible to present a doctrine of the Trinity (as a clear alternative to Athanasius) which would preserve the transcendent 'alterity' of God, affirm the reality of the indwelling God and the creative power of God's Spirit at work in the world and recognise salvation not as the result of a bloody sacrifice made by Jesus on the Cross (however existentially rich in symbolic significance (29)), but in consequence of our travelling the inward journey of the life of Grace and discovering for ourselves the mysterious and wondrous resources of the human soul. Jesus, as the Christa, would then symbolise, like the Buddha, the ideal of the truly enlightened person who has made this journey and, losing the self, discovered who they really were; thus becoming in our world, a light to enlighten all who will walk by it - the Logos incarnate.

This would not at all make Jesus a figure of insignificance. On the contrary, to those who turn to him for inspiration (as to the Buddha), his life and teachings are a continuous source of enlightenment, astonishment and deep delight. His sayings and stories, the paradigm of his life, speak ever more richly to mind and heart as the years go by. The integrity of person, the incredible matching of life and language challenge to the core of our being. Who can but admire his example in speaking out for the poor and despised, the underprivileged and socially unacceptable people of his day; his liberal, open attitudes towards women; his compassion; and his single-minded courage in risking his life for a new way of understanding our relationship with God and creation? He is, assuredly, amongst the greatest of the children of God; a beautiful poetic genius who lived out the wisdom he taught.

Jesus the Christ becomes so much more significant as a real, human person; more inspiring and convincing as another human being, struggling with God and humanity as we do, rather than as a god whose humanity is consequently a facade, quite different from ours. The way to Salvation, wholeness of person, is revealed in the paradigm of the life and teachings of Jesus. Its flower is the experience of union or nirvana, where we shed the delusions of time and separateness.

The doctrine of the Trinity is so much more meaningful and challenging when applied not exclusively to Jesus of Nazareth, but, as Augustine taught in The Trinity (30), used as a dynamic model descriptive both of the Nature of God and of the psyche of every human being. The incarnation is true then, as Martineau declared, not of Jesus exclusively, but of all humanity universally. That same Christ/a, made manifest in Jesus, indwells us all, offering each one of us the same possibility of union with God, described by Scholastics, such as Saint John of the Cross, as the Hypostatical Union of the soul with God; in this life, difference within unity.

Clearly, each human being, whilst essentially one person, possesses many personnae. I adopt a different persona in different relationships - with my intimates, with my colleagues, with my children, with my parents, with my dentist; in phantasy and reality, unconsciously and wittingly - but remain one person. So God, whilst also able to adopt not merely three, but, as it seems to the student of comparative religious experience, many personnae, remains essentially One.

A fascinating account of the relationships between the Persons of the Trinity - the Trinity as a psychodynamic model for the Nature of God - is given by another late contemporary of Coleridge, the brilliant nineteenth century thinker, Philip Henry Wicksteed (31), (for a time minister at Old Chapel, Dukinfield) in *The Reactions Between Dogma and Philosophy*, where Wicksteed elaborates the thought of Aquinas. Wicksteed wrote:

> The 'Word' then proceeds from the 'intellective power' in the being of God, and its content is God himself. We distinguish between the powers of our minds and our minds themselves, but this is only because we cannot grasp the essential being and nature of our minds. In God we must suppose the 'intellective power', that begets the 'Word', to be no other than his very self or essence. But if I think of myself, my thought is distinguishable from the intellective power which begets it, and the distinction asserts itself to me as something 'real', that actually is, however completely identical the thought and the thinker (who is also the object of the thought) may be. Our minds cannot choose but carry up this sense of a real distinction into our conception of intelligence as such, and it in no way qualifies our sense of unity. Thus both a distinction and a relation, between the source of thought and the thought, a kind of paternity and sonship, necessarily enters into our conception of deity ...

The 'Word' proceeds from its Divine Source, says Wicksteed, and a real intrinsic relation distinguishes them from each other. Yet they are like, not with the imperfect likeness of an earthly parent and child, but with the perfect and essential unity of identity and substance.

LOVE AND DECONSTRUCTION

The Face in the Abyss is the Face of Love. As Timothy Leary writes in his commentary on the Tibetan Book of the Dead, *Psychedaelic Experience* (32), the ecstasy of the First Bardo, intitiated in his experiments with psychotomimetic drugs, is dominated by the feeling of intense love. As one's individuality and autonomy of movement disappear and one's control is "surrendered to the total organism" every cell in one's body "sings the song of freedom". But then the Ego recognises it is being swallowed up by the ecstasy, disappearing into the unity, falling into the Abyss, and is beset by terror; fearing the loss of encapsulation "in the structure of ego and tribe." Through "panic and a desire to latch on to the familiar ... the potentiality to move from one level of consciousness to another is gone. Your fear and desire to control have driven you to settle for one static site of consciousness."

If language is the most effective weapon of encapsulation in defending the dominance of the Divine Father's macho world, the most effective weapon against that macho world, in deconstructing the power of received language, is love and its acolyte, sexual desire. Which is why tyrannies are at such pains to control and inhibit love and sensuality and to promote a ruthless form of censorship. It is, as I shall argue later, why all that is feminine is despised and women are subjugated. The frailer the boundaries of the Ego system, the more ruthlessly are the mores held with violence against the individual, against difference. People who seek out power, control and status are in flight from their own psychic vulnerability, which is surely why so many schizoidal individuals gain political power - their ambition is fuelled by the vertigo of freedom; the terror of 'being no-one at all'.

The soul has its own geography - boundaries and 'beyond'. We speak of falling in love. This is the opposite kind of Fall to the Hebrew/Christian Fall, which was *'superbia'* - a Fall upwards into the cardinal sin of Pride. The Fall of love takes us down, leads the way into a regression to the Shadow side of the Void, against which civilisation and our identities are built.

THE DREAM

And what of the language of the dream - Freud's Royal Road into the Unconscious? The dreaming world stands at the interface between self and Self; between the Ego and the Other; between the Persona and the Abyss. Although the Ego construct is still as intact in the dreaming world as in the relationship with the overt world, it has a greater freedom to deconstruct within the imaginary, thrown world of the dream's symbolic structures. Through our dreams we may converse with the Other, prepare the way for the Ego's regressive descent into the Abyss, confront the archetypes and explore existential worlds unavailable to our waking consciousness.

The inherent trace consciousness of language conditions all psychic experience for Derrida, from deep sleep to dreams to ordinary awareness and even to mystical experiences. Language provides the inescapable mode for our experience of reality. The Buddhist philosopher, Nagarjuna, by contrast (33), takes the "inherent nature of language in its subject-object conceptualizing of all experience to be the major obstacle to the experience of the real."

To go from inscribed trace (i.e. writing) to spoken word and the arche-writing "that prefigures and predisposes both," writes Coward (34), "only to be thrown back again, in a continual deconstructive reverse, would seem to be Derrida's use of language as a means for spiritual realization." The language we are deconstructing, writes Derrida, is our own - our own consciousness. We are ourselves the text we are deconstructing, which is why, as he says, nothing exists outside of the text. Deconstruction of language is the process of becoming self-aware, of self-realization.

Psychodynamic therapists, following Freud and Jung, see the interpretation of dreams, similarly, as a process of personal deconstruction - of psyche analysis - in which Primary or Id (arche) language is revealed in the dream content - both latent and manifest - and engaged by the Dreaming Ego. The conscious Ego, centre of the Secondary Thought Processes, converses with the Primary Thought Processes through meditation on the dream. A continuous deconstructive reversal is encouraged by this process.

Rhadakrishnan (35), commenting on his translation of the Bhagavadgita, says those who "live on the surface of life may not feel the distress, the laceration of spirit", which comes to the hero of the Gita, Arjuna. Life's anxieties touch him with gnawing distress as he "sinks into the gulf of utter blackness" which inevitably comes to those who look deeply within themselves. "If the divine truth," he writes, "which is free of access to all mankind, is attained only by a few, it shows that only a few are willing to pay the price for it."

In the language of the Primary Thought Processes Arjuna is making his 'descent'. Dreams may portray, even caricature, the hurry and scurry of life, the Ego's restless absorption in the fulfilment of the mores, its incessant struggle to gain worth and control, hold on to itself, by flight to the 'Up' world; by height rather than depth; by lightness rather than weight. A failure to deconstruct and a continuous absorption in the 'Up' world leads to a dangerous flight into phantasy and rationalisation. Like Icarus in the Primary, archetypal world of myth, the flight comes to disastrous end as the Sun, archetypal symbol of the Arche - melts our waxen wings.

Up is the light world - Down is the heavy world - down in the dumps - up on a high! The word guru means 'a heavy or weighty person'. In *The Unbearable Lightness of Being* (36), Milan Kundera wrote: "The heaviest of burdens crushes us, we sink beneath it, it pins us to the ground." But "in the love poetry of every age" we long "to be weighed down" by our lover's body:

> The heaviest of burdens is therefore simultaneously an image of life's most intense fulfilment. The heavier the burden, the closer our lives come to the earth, the more real and truthful they become. Conversely, the absolute absence of a burden causes us to be lighter than air, to soar into the heights, take leave of the earth and our earthly being, and become only half real, our movements as free as they are insignificant.

Regression takes us down, heavily, towards what we most desire - Love, the Good Breast, the Liminal Space of the Eternal Feminine - but also to what we most fear - freedom. Which is why, as I shall argue in following chapters, the more right wing the political or theological regime, the more overt control it will bring to bear on sexuality, especially on deviance; the more it will press for rigid adherence to family mores, however crippling these are of people, and especially of women. Living 'high' and not 'down to earth' such leaders, taking with boring regularity the high moral ground of the Moral Right, lose touch with reality and with humanity. Their influence in the world is not on the side of the Great Healer, but of the Great Divider, providing a manic milieu, unnaturally severed from that Ground of Being, which reaches out from the Non-Being, eternal fountain of Life and Love. Deviance becomes, then, the covert, often unwitting, agent of deconstruction - unlikely ally to the Holy Spirit.

The 'gender feminists'(37) are, for these reasons, right to point out that equality is not enough. Equality of opportunity may mean simply an even more powerful reassertion - equally now by women and men - of the masculine values (equal as equal to men), not balanced by feminine values, cementing even more assuredly their Patriarchal macho grip on our hierarchical, highly competitive, materially greedy world. As Kate Millett wrote in her *Sexual Politics* (38), modern society is deeply patriarchal, riddled with the politics of "sexual dominion" and suffused with "phallocentric" thinking. We need to work towards the creation of a culture where difference is not merely tolerated, but encouraged, and where we may be held whilst we fall towards the Abyss, the dark fecundity of our inner being, to rediscover who and what we are. Equity will, then, follow naturally from the creative marriage of archetypal gender values as they find expression in individuals and their communities. The fight for sexual equality, clearly, must still be fought, but now against the background of that new, postmodernist revolution taking place in our world as we approach the millenium, where we see the dynamic stirrings of the Eternal Feminine, The Goddess Re-Awakening (39), bringing *jouissance* in her train.

NOTES FOR CHAPTER ONE - THE ABYSS

1. Lacan, J. *Ecrits*, Tavistock. 1977. Pp 1-7
2. *The Hysterical Male,* ed. Arthur and Marie Louise Kroker. Macmillan. 1991. P. 227
3. Derrida, J. *Writing and Difference* tr. Bass,A. Routledge.   1990 ed. P. 8
4. John 3 v 1-11
5. Note Edward Schillebeeckx. *Jesus.* Collins. 1979. P. 197: The New Testament reveals a Jesus whose "earthly mission is that of the 'Son of David' to Israel", whilst only at the Resurrection "is he revealed by God as 'the universal Christ'".
6. Luke 9, v 24
7. *The Cloud of Unknowing*, ed. McCann, J. with commentary by Fr. Augustine Baker. Burns Oates. 1952 ed. Pp 13 and 218.
8. Derrida, J. *Writing and Difference.* tr.Bass,A.   Routledge. 1990 ed. 'Force & Signification',   P. 7
9. Derrida ibid. Pp. 79 ff.
10. Jean-Luc Marion. *God Without Being.* 1991 Chicago. Cf. also Jacques Derrida. *The Gift Of Death.* Chicago.1995.P.55: "What is it that makes us tremble in the mysterium tremendum? It is the gift of infinite love, the dis symmetry that exists between the divine regard that sees me, and myself, who doesn't see what is looking at me."
11. St. John of the Cross. tr. Peers, A. Complete Works, Vol. 1. Burns Oates. P. 422.
12. Guntrip, H. *Schizoid Penomena, Object Relations and the Self.* Hogarth.1968, P. 218
13. Julia Kristeva. *Tales of Love.* Columbia. 1987.Pp. 23-4; and Heidegger,M. *What Is Called Thinking?*, tr. Wieck, F.D., Harper and Row. 1968. P. 227.
14. Heidegger, M. *Heidegger: Basic Writings.* ed. Krell,D. Harper and Row. 1977, P. 385.
15. Julia Kristeva, *Tales of Love.* 'Stabat Mater'. Pp. 234 ff.Columbia. 1987.
16. Coward, H. *Derrida and Indian Philosophy* Sri Satguru Publications. 1991.
17. Just as Logos is God's Self-consciousness in creation for the Greek tradition, speaking to the one who climbs the darkness of the Cave towards the Light of Reality.
18. Socrates also down-graded the written over the oral. Reliance on writing does not impart wisdom, he declared, but serves only as a reminder. Reliance on writing will lead, inevitably, to memory loss.
19. See Longxi, Z. *The Tao and the Logos.* P. 391; and Cassirer, E., Language

and Myth, tr. Langer, S.K. Dover Books. 1953. P. 7

20.   Derrida,J. *Writing and Difference* Ibid.P. 67
21.   Stevens, Wallace. *Collected Poems*.Faber and Faber.1954. P. 9
22.   See Perkins, M.A., *Coleridge's Philosophy*. Oxford. 1994
23.   Perkins Ibid. Pp. 50ff.
24.   Jacques Derrida, in *The Gift of Death* (Chicago Press. 1995 Pp. 26/7) argues that "heresy always marks a difference or departure, keeping itself from what is publicly or commonly declared" is not only "in its very possibility, the essential condition of responsibility; paradoxically, it also destines responsibility to the resistance or dissidence of a type of secrecy", i.e. mystery. The exercise of responsibilty, he writes, "seems to leave no choice but this one, how ever uncomfortable it may be, of paradox, heresy, and secrecy." Further, "there is no responsibility without a dissident and inventive rupture with respect to tradition, authority, orthodoxy, rule, or doctrine."
25.   Rhadakrishnan,S. *The Bhagavadgita*.Allen & Unwin. 1963 ed. Pp. 26/7
26.   Jung, C.G. Complete Works. Vol 11. Routledge. 1958. Pp.107 ff.
27.   Perkins Ibid. P. 65
28.   Jung. Ibid. P. 157
29.   Jacques Derrida, in *The Gift Of Death*. Chicago. 1995. Pp. 57ff., comments on the implications of the fact that three great religions trace their origins to Abraham, a man who (like God with Christ) was ready to murder his own son.

Abraham presents himself to God, in secret, and suddenly all ethical considerations are turned on their head. A new order of responsibility asserts itself - a choice has to be made between his inner vision and family, community values. His duty as a father means he must protect Isaac; his duty as a citizen also. But his faith requires him to be ready to break with duty. The tale is reminiscent of the hard saying of Jesus: "If any one comes to me and does not hate his own father and mother and his wife and children and brothers and sisters, yes, and even his own life, he cannot be my disciple.(Lk.14,26) (Creed suggests this is hyperbole of Mt.10, 35-39: "he who loveth father, mother, son or daughter more than me." Or even his own psyche!)

What sort of demand is this? That I shall love God more than anything dear and near to me? If I put to death what I hate it is no sacrifice; I must sacrifice, even betray, what I love. Give up love to love. Abraham must love Isaac to the point where he will offer him to God, "grant him death" - actually reveal his love by commiting what ethics will call murder. Any court, any judge and jury would condemn Abraham as insane for this terrible act - a deviant monster beyond the pale, cutting his trusting son's throat and burning the body.

Consider the actual place where the sacrifice was to take place. It is where Solomon built the Temple, where the Grand Mosque of Jerusalem stood, from where Muhammed in Islamic legend mounted his horse for paradise after his death; close to the Wailing Wall and the Way of the Cross. A holy place radically, rabidly, fiercely, barbarically in dispute between these three great monotheisms; who have fought over it, made war with fire and blood, each claiming its particular perspective and claiming an original historical and political interpretation of Messianism and the sacrifice of Isaac.

Many Christians have seen the story as a foreshadowing of the sacrifice God made by murdering His own Son, the Christ, on a Cross erected close to this self-same spot where Abraham was ready to murder his son. The sacrifice of the Christ has also been understood as necessary to human freedom, representing the giving up in love of that which is loved. The sacrifice is the sacrifice of any patriarchal implications of paternity; giving freedom to err, freedom to be different; a protection against conformity and mere submission. The sacrifice of the Christ, in love and through love, preserves human difference and spiritual choice before the demands of the Other. By giving up (sacrificing) our children to the Other, their own potentiality, their own Core, we give them the freedom which holds us in love. If we do not make this sacrifice we lose our children and they may lose their own opportunity to relate freely to the Other, no matter how, through the conventions, we may create a love that is binding between us; i.e. based not on difference, but on complicity.

It is impossible not to be struck by the absence of a woman in this monstrous story. Is this simply the masculine hierarchical patriarchy of the culture? Or is there at the very basis of the story the exclusion or sacrifice of woman? Is it even that it is the hierarchical relationship, the passing on of that hierarchy through father and son which must be sacrificed? Is it patriarchy itself that must be sacrificed with its nationalistic, competitive, ruthlessness?

30.   Augustine. tr. Burnaby, J. *Augustine: Later Works*. SCM.1955.Pp.17 ff.
31.   Wicksteed, P.H. *The Reactions Between Dogma and Philosophy* Williams and Norgate. 1920. P. 271
32.   Leary, T. *Psychedelic Experience*. Academy Editions. 1964.Pp.36/7
33.   Coward,H. Ibid. P.135
34.   Coward, H. Ibid. P. 140
35.   Rhadakrishnan. Ibid P. 51

36.   Milan Kundera. *The Unbearable Lightness of Being*. tr. Heim, M.H.
        Faber and Faber. 1987 ed.   P. 5
37.   Sommers, C.H. *Who Stole Feminism*. Simon and Schuster. 1994.
38.   Millett,K. *Sexual Politics*. Doubleday. 1969.
39.   See Nicholson, S. *The Goddess Re-Awakening*. Quest Books. 1989.

CHAPTER TWO

SEXUAL DESIRE:

ACOLYTE OF HOLINESS

In the happy night, in secret, when none saw me, nor I beheld naught, without light or guide, save that which burned in my heart.

This light guided me more surely than the light of noonday to the place where he (well I knew who!) was awaiting me. A place where none appeared.

Oh, night that guided me, oh, night more lovely than the dawn, Oh night that joined Beloved with lover, Lover transformed in the Beloved!

Upon my flowery breast, kept wholly for himself alone, there he stayed sleeping, and I caressed him, and the fanning of the cedars made a breeze.

The breeze blew from the turret as I parted his locks; with his gentle hand he wounded my neck and caused all my senses to be suspended.

I remained, lost in oblivion; My face I reclined on the Beloved. All ceased and I abandoned myself, leaving my cares forgotten among the lilies.

> John of the Cross
> *Dark Night of the Soul*

So now the beloved is in love, but with what he cannot tell. He does not know and cannot explain what has happened to him; he is like a man who has caught an eye infection from another and cannot account for it; he does not realise that he is seeing himself in his lover as in a glass.

> Plato
> *Phaedrus*

Charity rising
from the vast abyss
past the stars above
abounds in all worlds,
unbounded love,
and with spousal kiss
disarms the sky-king.

Hildegard of Bingen
Symphonia

Man makes himself man in order to be God, and selflessness considered from this point of view can appear to be an egoism; but precisely because there is no common measure between human reality and the self-cause which it wants to be, one could just as well say that we lose ourselves in order that the self-cause may exist. We will consider then that all human existence is a passion ...

Jean Paul Sartre
Being and Nothingness

Sexual desire is the recognition of a movement towards a mystery - the mystery of the Other Person and the mystery of one's own inner Self. Perversion springs from the common condition of being trapped in the desire or quest for the adventure and discovery, the spontanaeity and freshness involved in the mystery, whilst at the same time holding back from the commitment and involvement (deep engagement) required by the mystery if it is to reveal itself. All forms of sexual desire, including those condemned by the community as deviant or perverted, represent a search - no matter how unconscious, no matter how often aborted - for one's own gender, identity and self-fulfilment. The ultimate goal of sexual desire, its telos, is a deconstruction culminating in union with the self-cause, even when the person is continually misfed by the manner in which the Ego acts out that desire. The desire here, revealed as sexual desire, is Love's desire to be complete, re-united. The desire is the desire of the Acorn to be an Oak. It is the desire which is towards a wish-fulfilment, when the wish is, as in Freud, *Wunst,* i.e. an Id wish, not an Ego wish; a wish from our potentia, a wish to be God, of such intensity it will brave the Abyss in order to be God.

Since the Ego approaches any activity, including sexual activity, from within the prison of its own conditioning, its own constructed sense of identity, and projects into that activity the unresolved psychodynamic problems of its relationship with the inner world of the psyche, sexual desire is deflected from its proper and natural goal - the goal of union, self-fulfilment or wholeness/holiness. Sartre described this dilemma of the Ego (as agent of the For-Itself) in Being and Nothingness (1). In 'normal' sexuality, he says, the Ego inevitably approaches sexual activity sadistically or masochistically. All 'normal' sexuality is sadomasochistic.

Sartre is commonly interpreted as having declared that all sexuality is a perversion, but he was making an ontological rather than a moral statement - a statement about the nature of our mode of being. Sexual desire, for Sartre, is not a perversion *per se*, but desire becomes perverted in the sexual act when the Ego or construct self uses sexual opportunity as a self-defence (a defence of the internal status quo) rather than as a vehicle of authenticity, a counter to the Ego's Bad Faith and Denial. Sexuality always entertains the possibility of perversion in the sense of 'turning from the way'; the possibility of deviating from the norm towards freedom.

Sartre describes the many ways human beings 'in love' attempt to possess, enslave, idolise and identify with their loves and the inevitable sterility of these attempts. Love as an enterprise of 'self' projection and 'self' reconstruction will inevitably provoke conflict and is doomed, he says, to disillusionment. Always human beings are in relation to the Other. A basic split appears in our nature, gnawing at us and pressing for restored unity (*dikaiosune* - righteousness or restoration). In the lover we hope to discover that unity, that self-restoration. This is, however, says Sartre, a forlorn hope. Behind the desire for unity lies the unrealisable goal of the union of the For-Itself and the In-Itself - realisable only in death; that is, in the absence of the For-Itself. God, the self-cause, represents this unrealisable union (2):

> Thus the best way to conceive of the fundamental project of human reality is to say humans are the beings whose project is to be God. Whatever may be the myths and the rites of the religion considered, God is first 'sensible to our hearts' as the one who identifies and defines us in his ultimate and fundamental project. If we possess a pre-ontological comprehension of the being of God, it is not the great wonders of nature nor the power of society which have conferred it upon us. God, value and supreme end of transcendence, represents the permanent limit in terms of which we make known to ourselves what we are. To be human means to reach towards being God. Or if you prefer, we are fundamentally the desire to be God.

This union of the In-Itself (the Ground of our existence) and the For-Itself (individual existence arising out of that Ground) is, says Sartre, a project that represents the desire for pure, objectless consciousness. In his struggles to avoid falling into the dualistic description of the psyche, which any 'I-Thou' topography inevitably involves, Sartre's writings are intriguingly reminiscent of the exposition of the Vedanta made by Shankara. Shankara also defines the quest for the Ground of Being, Brahman, as a desire for pure, unreflective consciousness and engages in the same philosophical issues.

In all ages and climes philosophical theologians have, of course, struggled with the dualism posed by the notion of the union of the soul with God. Philosophers are offended by the dualism of the 'I-Thou' experience and yet the desired monism cannot be reached without abolishing either the 'I' or the 'Thou' - or so it seems. Zaehner, however, in *Concordant Discord* (3) points out that what is impossible for the logician is not impossible for the lover. He quotes the Muslim sage, Ibn Tufayl, who declared that whilst unity predominates in the experience of union with God, to interpret this as absolute identity is a 'misguided conceit'. Both the author of the *Bhagavad Gita* and the *Saiva Siddhanta*, says Zaehner, would agree with Tufayl that where there is love there must be both duality and unity. Incomprehensible to the intellect, it is self-evident to the lover.

The *Brhadaranyaka Upanishad* (IV.3.21) declares that as in the arms of a beloved man or woman one knows nothing more of the outward or the inner, in the human person embraced by the all-knowing absolute, all longings are fulfilled, only the longing for the absolute subsists, all desire and sorrow disappear.

The union of lovers as an analogy for the union of the soul with God was used also in Mediaeval and Renaissance Christendom. It is represented, for example, in the *Picta Poesis* of Barthelemy Aneau (4), where lovers are united by a true androgynous lovers' knot and have become one with the Cross, represented by the Tree of Life. In mystical love-lyrics the world over, amongst Taoist poets from China, Shamans from Siberia, Christians from Europe, the poet sighs and faints before a higher, profounder aspect of her own self; expressing a passionate ardour in language that is frankly erotic. The Psyche (as in the Greek myth) becomes female in the presence of the male Eros: an androgynous union takes place to resolve a basic split in human nature.

Despite the fact that the Pope and the Church represented, in classical Christian teaching, the androgynous union or marriage of Christ and the Church (the Bride of Christ in Christian myth), theologians like Scotus Erigena, who openly expounded the concept of androgyny, of internal union or 'spiritual marriage' with God, did so only by defying the ban of the church. It was, for example, the exposition of the hypostatical union of the soul with God, the marriage of the soul with God, which brought St.John of the Cross and Meister Eckhart before the Inquisition. The notion of androgyny took them into deep and perilous theological waters.

The basic split in human nature, which the experience of union was expected to heal, is described by contemplatives as a rift between the individual soul and the Ground of Existence or as a schism within the individual psyche. This schism is healed, the contemplatives taught, in the ecstasy of Love; the healing and restorative agent is Love - in the West called Eros (as in Freud) or the Holy Spirit. The presence of this restorative or reparative agent to consciousness is recorded as (sexual) desire - whether the object of that desire is God, Christ, Krishna, Allah or a sexual partner.

Sex in the etymological sense of division existed in our universe long before copulation. Creatures divided in order to reproduce before genitalia evolved. Life has always sought completion, fulfilment and perpetuation (immortality). God, as immanent Persona God, alive in the very Fundus of the psyche, remains essentially sexual or erotic in this sense, seeking through Love fulfilment, perpetuation, self-consciousness and the resolution of duality.

Dualism as an alienated, fallen state, is represented in the Biblical myths from the beginning in the myth of Adam and Eve. Adam is the archetypal androgyne, from whom Eve is split as a separate duality in his world. She appears from his left side, which in myth and the underworld of dreams is the female side of intuition, of dark fecundity. In the *unio coniunctioris* of sexual intercourse the split is resolved in a union that finds expression in the birth of a child. This child may be the flesh and blood child, gestating in the womb, or it may be a spiritual child, a symbol of new life, appearing in the dreams of the lovers - archetype of the Logos or the Christ/a Child.

Within the *Kabbalah* Jewish contemplatives also developed these androgynous themes independently of the Christians. The *Zohar*, for example, teaches how the original unity of God and Creation was broken; how the *Shekinah* became exiled in the world, wandering lost and incomplete. The goal of the religious life, for the *Kabbalah* and the whole raison d'etre of existence, is the reunification of God and Creation - i.e. the *En Sof* and the *Shekinah*. This restored unity is called *Yichud*. Once again it is Love that resolves this separation and the destiny of every soul is to know this Love and to return to the Source from which it emanates.

PRIMARY AND SECONDARY NARCISSISM

Modern depth psychology, too, conceives of a basic split at the root of human nature. In Freudian, Jungian and Existentialist psychodynamic theory the psyche is an essential unity that splits or fragments early in our experience. The split is seen as a traumatic event, devastatingly difficult for the self to endure, arising in the movement from non-differentiation to differentiation. The infant leaves behind an experience of the world (including umbilical cord, breast, mother and the child's own body) as an undivided unity, for an experience of being separated out from the world - even from one's own body. The sense of being in this particular body develops for most of us by the time we are two and a half years old, along with our use of the language by which the construct self is defended. But some people never quite develop a firm sense of embodiment, a well-defined Body Ego. They remain, even in adult life, somewhat disembodied.

The original non-differentiation between self and not-self within the infant is described by Freud as Primary Narcissism. The separate, differentiated self emerging from the weaning process is further split by the socialising of the infant, whereby some aspects of the infant's affective and behavioural life are acceptable to the caretaking figures in the environment and some are not. Social training produces an Ego Ideal, an image of "what I ought to be". Secondary Narcissism represents the self-absorption of the split-off-self or Ego as it attempts to maintain self-regard by fulfilling the demands of the Ego Ideal (Oedipal Expectations). In a paper on Narcissism, written in 1914, Freud wrote (5):

> The development of the ego consists in a departure from the primary narcissism and results in a vigorous attempt to recover it. This departure is brought about by means of the displacement of libido to an ego-ideal imposed from without, while gratification is derived from the attainment of this ideal.

The psychopathology of the neuroses, hysterias and psychoses arises out of a spiritual strugggle. This struggle is a spontaneous attempt to heal the psyche and to restore lost unity or integrity. The desire for lost unity reveals itself with less potency amongst so-called 'normal' people, but according to contemplative teaching, that desire, however hidden, is present in us all. All our hearts are, as Augustine had it, restless until they find their rest in God.

Freud pointed out that we seek lost aspects of ourselves in our lovers. Falling 'in love' reflects the desire for integration or completeness, for lost unity. Sexual desire becomes the agent of the integrative process. It is the desire for the Other; for that within me (now projected onto my lover) which will fulfil me and make me whole (holy). Sexual desire is thus the desire for my deconstructed Self. When I project this desire I see myself in my lover as in a glass. The lover becomes as God to me. I am infected and infused with a desire that moves towards the Other, caught in the image of the one I love.

Psychotherapy conducted at depth pursues a regressive programme taking the analysand back through various life crises or psychosexual stages (adolescence, puberty, latency, Oedipal, depressive, schizoidal) to the original unity of the psyche. The contemplative teachers of the various world religions appear to describe the same journey and the same goal.

Francis Tustin in *Autism and Childhood Psychosis* (6), writes of the difficulties we experience in moving from the infantile state of non-differentiation into a sense of separateness: "the complexity and delicacy of the time-consuming process of becoming aware of the world and its objects, persons and other minds." The child who receives very inadequate nurturing at this critical period of mental development may adopt autistic behaviour as a defence against the excruciatingly painful hazards of this crucial step:

> the infant has to learn to tolerate the fact that outside people do not always pattern themselves in terms of blissful completion of instinctual activities. He has to learn to bear 'divine discontent'. In a good rearing situation, blissful satisfaction occurs often enough for good 'linking' to become part of the infant's developing experience. Mutual satisfactions bridge the gap between mother and infant. As we have seen from the clinical material, if for any reason the gap is not so bridged, deathly terrors rush in.

Inadequate nurturing or abandonment at this phase of development leads to an inner feeling of 'not being held', lodging in the psyche as a terror of a dreadful 'fall' into a dark, bottomless hole - into the Abyss (*Abgrund*). But even those infants who have 'good-enough-mothers', as Winicott put it, find this movement from non-differentiation to differentiation a severe hazard. Francis Tustin believes we all come into adulthood with a 'pocket' of autism, revealing itself in our life style. She points out how some "relatively normal and often extremely talented people" treat other people, objects and institutions as if they were pawns on the chessboard of their self-centred purposes. People with false pretensions, people who are social chameleons, people who take over the ideas of others lock, stock and barrel and use them dogmatically or chaotically, are also manipulating the 'outside world' to cloak their vulnerability. Authentic people, capable of genuine caring and of really creative and imaginative behaviour must, she writes, have come to terms with their own 'pocket' of autism by enduring (7):

> the heart-break which is at the centre of human existence, which has to be experienced again and again in ever-widening contexts of developing maturity.

THE AUTISTIC POCKET

It is fruitful to transpose the concept of an 'autistic pocket' into contemplative theology. Autism is a term used to describe children and adults who are caught (sometimes it seems entirely) in their own thought processes, their own image-making. But whilst autism is a condition which may incapacitate people for ordinary living, 'normal' people also reveal the presence of the 'autistic pocket' inasmuch as they are usually quite unable to still their thought processes. The majority of us are trapped in image-making - as Derrida has it, language thinks us. We even identify ourselves with our own thought processes so that our sense of self is intimately conjoined with our own image-making, especially the 'language-tapes', which continuously engage the focal point of consciousness, flowing in an incessant stream of 'free-associative' and self-precipitating programmes.

Most people do not see this identification as a problem and do not believe their thought processes are an obstacle to personal development. But, of course, this is exactly how the contemplatives do view our absorption in image-making - as an obstacle. Contemplative prayer in all the great religions - amongst the Buddhists, the Sufi, the Christians and the Jews - affirms the ancient exhortation (8): "Be still and know that I am God." Contemplative prayer is a technique for stilling the mind, for controlling, containing and eventually extinguishing all imagery, especially the imagery of words.

Release from the bondage of images produces, we are told, a state of non-differentiation! In these states of pure consciousness, of pre-reflective cognition, the false self is surrendered and an internal union (yoga) takes place between the otherwise sundered poles of the psyche. The two fundamental delusions of life are thus removed - the delusion of separateness and the delusion of time. Now where else in human experience are these two delusions unknown, except in ecstasy and in the unweaned child? They are unknown to Primary Narcissism, characterised, as Freud said, by the Oceanic feeling - in the Abyss. The delusions of separateness and time (as opposed to the unity of the Eternal Now) emerge in weaning on the other side of the autistic trap. The integrative process takes us from the Many to the One, that we may take again that hazardous journey with, hopefully, a more satisfactory resolution: back from the One to the Many, creating a viable ferry between the two worlds.

Therapeutic endeavour informs us that where anger reveals itself despair is close to hand; where despair reveals itself anger is close to hand. They are complementary twins. Just as anxiety may be a defence against massive fear, so despair and anger may be defences against a terror of abandonment and confusion (*confundus* - without foundation). This abandonment may be conceived as a pit, an abyss, a bottomless hole, a void, and may be represented in this way in one's dreams. The threat of abandonment appears to the Ego as a 'death', in presenting what is the ultimate psychic threat from the point of view of the established Ego - identity loss or soullessness. The Ego does not believe in pure, unreflective consciousness. It believes in and trusts in its own ability to hold itself together within its image-making, language-dominated world. Faith, in the sense of complete, committed trust to an 'inner ruler of the psyche' is madness to the Ego. It is not aware of its own ultimate psychic indestructibility - i.e. the indestructibility of deconstructed consciousness, as opposed to that of the Ego construct. An absence of imagery presents a Nothingness which is the Pit to the Ego. It does not recognise that consciousness remains as a consciousness of Nothingness. The Ego is not encouraged by the words of Jesus (9): "He who loses his self (psyche) will save his self." The Ego is unpersuaded by the paradigm of the Life of the Christ/a, which teaches we must first die in order to be born again. The Ego is motivated by an engram - a terrifying memory of separation and of a painful struggle to meet the demands of the Ego Ideal against internal sanctions implying failure would mean further abandonment. It does not recognise Nothingness as a desired spiritual goal - a restoration of unity and peace - but as a horror to be avoided at all cost.

Sexual desire, however, reaches towards this unity and peace, this Nothingness, towards an ecstasy - an *ekstasis*, a standing outside of one's self. Ecstasy requires soullessness. It is the handmaid of union, non-separation, non-division. The Marriage Ceremony in the Book of Common Prayer calls marriage an "excellent mystery, that in it is signified and represented the spiritual marriage and unity betwixt Christ and his Church". St. Paul's letter to the Ephesians (Ch. V) is quoted, where husbands are exhorted to love their wives as Christ loved the Church and wives to be subject to husbands as the Church is to Christ. Setting aside issues concerning the actual authenticity of these passages attributed to Paul and their male chauvinism, it is possible to recognise the clear reference back to the androgyne Adam in the quotation from *Genesis* (II, v 24) found in *Ephesians* (V) and repeated in the marriage ceremony:

> Therefore a man leaves his father and his mother and cleaves to his wife, and they become one flesh.

The sex act promises, physically and spiritually, a union - an ecstasy of self-loss. The penis becomes an umbilical cord, a tube of flesh joining two bodies. Sexual problems between partners so often reflect an inability to reach self-loss; i.e. they reveal an absence of faith - the inability to let go, be penetrated, risk commitment, lose control, be possessed. When the sex act is over and the partners sever the umbilical cord yet again by the withdrawal of the penis (or its surrogates), they are thrown onto alternative devices by which to maintain the sense of a return to Mother, the sense of an affirmed self, which may yet hope for the Oedipal expectations to be realised.

It is difficult to 'let go' when you have chosen a partner (however unwittingly) precisely so that s/he will 'hold you up'. The sexual desire (representing unconsciously the Id wishes) is at odds with the desires of the Ego. The Ego desires the sexual partner to affirm the surface self, to reinforce its defences, to hold it in the delusional phantasy world of image-making. But the inevitable consequence of the pursuit of this desire is that the sexual act becomes one of mere masturbation, since the partner is being used to satisfy the phantasy world and its defences, rather than as someone with whom one might make an authentic and most intimate attempt to be genuine and free. Here, the wishes or desires of the Id are at variance with those of the Ego, since the Id desires that the sexual act shall represent an intercourse of persons, a confrontation with the Other, a genuine 'letting go' of barriers.

Sexual behaviour becomes a perversion of sexual desire, as Sartre wrote, when the Ego manipulates the sexual situation as a means of defence, of reconstruction, rather than respond to the invitation of Eros into an ecstasy. We may live by faith or by fear: faith here represents a choice to deconstruct in favour of Eros; whereas fear represents a choice to defend the self against Eros (a blasphemy against the Holy Spirit).

The conflict between the surface self and the unconscious Self creates a continual 'in-out' drama. Sexual partners try again and again to discover those things the socially conditioned Ego anticipates from their relationship. The failure of a partner to affirm or uphold leads, generally, to a withdrawal from relationship - perhaps into frigidity. Since the desire for affirmation is a projection from the Lost Child within the adult and is to be understood in terms of the past relationship of that Child to the internalised Parents, it is in fact quite impossible for either partner to meet the Child's demands. Each partner will be dissatisfied and disillusioned by the other. It is unlikely they will see the pain and conflict of their predicament as a spiritual opportunity to regress, to deconstruct, and assimilate their internal problems. They are not likely to see their domestic trauma as a means of paving the way to the 'safe inside' world of the unweaned infant. It is more likely they will look elsewhere for affirmation, for possibilities of reconstruction, and may turn to fresh partners or fall into one of the so-called deviancies.

The word deviancy implies there is a norm from which it is possible to deviate. In sexual matters, however, there are no norms, except those in people's imaginations. Freud shocked many Europeans when he wrote that children had sexual feelings. Sexual feelings amongst children were a deviancy from an accepted norm, perceiving children as sexless creatures. Recently, the British public have been shocked to discover how widespread is the sexual abuse of children within the community. That abuse is so wide-spread as to have become a norm amongst us. It is, however, especially difficult for people to acknowledge abuse as a 'norm', since we have wanted to believe that a norm must be both natural and healthy - indeed the words 'normal' and 'healthy' have been used synonymously amongst us for decades. Only with deep reluctance will people admit to a clearly unhealthy norm in the rather obvious evidence of our society's common and vast unease with intimacy.

The notion of deviancy has been applied to forms of sexual expression believed to exist only amongst a small minority of individuals offending against certain beliefs about what is and is not acceptable sexually at the public face of the community. But, since the Kinsey reports in the mid-century, we have known that a wide range of the sexual behaviour dubbed deviant, is commonly practised to one degree or another by most of us.

Gay people, in particular, have suffered from the stigma of deviance and so have people who have shared two or more partners. Divorce was a stigmatized deviance in the thirties, which could have cost a person his/her livelihood. By the seventies, of course, the accepted norm had become serial monogamy, where it was expected still that when a person leaves one partner for another, the partners will contain their sexual behaviour within the new relationship. In the 1900s the divorce rate was about 500 a year in a married population of around 11 million. By the late 1930s the annual divorce rate had increased to around 7,500 - less than one in 2,000. It is now moving towards one in two. Divorce, therefore, has become the 'norm'. Even within the Royal Family, set up publicly as a kind of idealised Holy Family, divorce is acceptable and may even become acceptable, now, upon the throne. It is ironic how the media has been caught in a hypocritical, holier than thou, presentation of 'shocking facts' about the Royal Family and notable Conservative politicians, when these 'shocking facts' are clearly epidemic amongst us.

THE ETERNAL TRIANGLE

All forms of sexual expression, heterosexual or homosexual, provide an opportunity for regression, appraisal and self-examination. Whereas some variations of sexual expression, such as fetishism, exhibitionism and paedaphilia, are obviously regressive in form, all our sexual involvement in fact invites us to regress and has regressive qualities about it, especially, for example in our foreplay and our use of language (sweetikins loves babywitzy, yes s/he does, hmmmm!). Sexual activity between partners, heterosexual or homosexual, always offers the possibility of pursuing the integrative path, since it challenges us to witness ourselves at our most intimate and vulnerable and to examine honestly the quality of the relationship and the roots of our involvement. Nothing is more revealing of us than our sexual interaction; so that what we had hoped to keep in the secret compartments of our souls, is, in our sexual lives, shouted from the rooftops.

If a client leaves a sexual partner whilst therapy is under way, the separation deprives the psychodynamic therapist of a significant therapeutic aid - the central transference in the client's life. The client will have transferred parental projections onto the partner and recreated childhood psychodynamics in that relationship. Many partners compromise with each other to protect against the rise of painful Child feelings by attempting to fulfil for each other the role of 'good' object. This assists them to maintain the Ego/Super-Ego liaison in each partner. They may, further, avoid disturbing that Ego/Super-Ego liaison (i.e. Child/Parent liaison) by leaving the moral and rational basis of their relationship unchallenged, unexamined. Some people remain within these comfortable, schizoidal compromises all their lives. But for many partners the aridity and lack of authentic creativity and growth within the compromise proves stultifying. The frustration and sense of disillusionment arising in response to the aridity takes the client directly into the Child's world and into the Child's sense of abandonment; and into the Child's rage at that abandonment.

The compromise the client has broken gives the therapist a core working tool. One has a kind of Transactional Workshop ready-made by the sexual relationship. Through this the therapist can assist the client to find, accept and assimilate his or her Lost Child and detach from the tyranny of the internalised Parent, which will have been transferred (conveniently for the therapist) onto the partner; and/or onto the therapist.

The client may take a new lover to find an object to transfer the powerful regressive Child desires for comfort - to love and be loved, to be held, to belong and feel at one with; a yearning for primary narcissism such as may overtake us violently in the anima/animus projections described by Jung.

In the triangular relationship between a person and two partners - the established partner and the new lover - the client may learn how to break projections and suffer the Child's pain, at the same time breaking the moral strictures, the deblitating source of guilt and shame, by working through the Child/Parent liaison. The triangle may provide the therapist with an alternative therapeutic workshop to the established sexual relationship. All three members may grow within it, if it is handled with sensitivity and genuine care on everyone's part.

The acceptability of the sexual relationship within the social mores bears no relationship to the therapeutic power such relationships may have for each partner. Ethel Person in *Love and Fateful Encounters* (10) remarks that some of the most transforming and positive sexual relationships are in fact adulterous ones. It's commonly assumed that adulterous love either fails of its own internal dynamics, or succeeds only by breaking up the marriages of its participants.   Her therapeutic experience has, however, led her to recognise that this is far from always the case. Moreover, she writes:

> one of the more 'satisfactory' forms of adulterous love is sometimes that in which the adulterous relationship endures over decades, forming a kind of stable triangle.

> From the perspective of the participants rather than from that of the observers,   these affairs may provide the sense of meaning, transcendence, immediacy of experience, and transformation that are the essence of any reciprocated love.

If, however, during therapy, one's client actually leaves an established partner it may often be difficult to avoid perceiving that action as a punishment of one or both parents for the abandonment experienced by the client as a child. The client is, it sometimes seems, seeking a fresh parent, a better breast. The client is abandoning the very situation most clearly revealing the consequences of the Child/Parent liaison. It may well be, however,   the new relationship comes to have its own validity and is deserving of respect even though it may represent yet another compromise between 'good' and 'bad' objects. Where a break has been made between the client and partner in favour of a new lover, the therapist will have to wait for the Parental projections to rise again in relationship to a new object; in this case, in all probability, the new lover (and/or, of course, within the therapeutic transference).

What has been fled in one relationship is likely to reassert itself in any new one. The opportunity to work through the central transference with the established partner and so assimilate and confront the Parent, through well-bearing of the empty-hopeless-despair of the Child, may merely have been postponed - perhaps indefinitely.

On the other hand the trauma of the break with our partner (and, perhaps, also with one's family) and the inevitable affront of the mores with subsequent moral acrimony from relatives and friends, may provide the grief and the conflict for an alternative opportunity to deconstruct, to make a bid for freedom, impossible within the original schizoid compromise of the relationship with the established partner.   The guilt, shame and conflict may themselves press the client into confrontation with the Parental imagos and lead to a detachment from the Parent's internal tyranny.   A consequence may also be the assimilation of the Child's abandonment feelings, since standing against the Parent brings the person under the Parental sanctions of abandonment (the 'No' of the Hero).   The trauma itself may then give the therapist an alternative Transactional Workshop.

The whole predicament is a veritable razor's edge.   Down one side is creative opportunity for growth and maturation and down the other side lies the real possibility of appalling destruction.   The Unconscious, Eros, however, is always ready to take this risk. It is concerned only for freedom and its own maturational purposes.   What may always be the critical element in the client in determining the outcome of these traumata, is whether in the end s/he is genuinely on the side of Eros, or whether s/he is simply plunging into an habitual inauthenticity in search of another breast.

A creative outcome will depend upon whether the person is on the side of Eros, or whether the revenge taken on the Parent in the form of the established partner is just too sweet to surrender!   Maturation may also be blocked by an isolation in the Child, which makes it too painful for the client to risk the overtures and promises made by Eros.   However, if we are to avoid the wrath of Eros in our lives, we must use our relationships for the sake of the purposes Eros requires in the growth of the Christ Child and the encounter with the more disinterested *Agape*, rather than use them for the purposes of perpetual consolation for the Lost Child.

THE FORM OF THE THIRD - EROS AND THE HOLY SPIRIT

John Haule, in *Divine Madness: Archetypes of Romantic Love* (11), discusses the psychodynamic implications of the myth of Lancelot and Guinevere, where, through their sexual involvement (though not apparently resented by Arthur), "Eros threatens to overbalance fealty". If, writes Haule, the Holy Spirit (that is the Third) is conducting this drama, we must conclude that God is countenancing adultery and endangering the kingdom. A Holy Spirit which can countenance the Queen's extramarital affair may well be able to countenance ours. Sometimes, Haule argues, such an affair may be "good for the marriage of the married party and for the psychological well-being and professional advancement of the single partner - although rarely without involving a good deal of work."

The affair may lead to the development of self-knowledge, a reassessment of one's values and especially to a new acquaintance with one's feelings. Most people, however, argues Haule, will, like Gawain, slip "unconsciously into entanglements" rather than follow the relationship, like Lancelot, in an unorthodox direction; for this requires a great deal of courage to face the guilt of offending the mores or hurting another human being. People naturally wish to be relieved of their feelings of guilt, but the relief of them removes their function as pointers to the tension "wherein the Third resides". We have to tolerate guilt so that we may grow strong enough to be free from the intimidation of the Super Ego, tolerate guilt long enough for it to speak to us, allowing us to discriminate the elements we have taken over unconsciously from family and society. The Third, claims Haule, is here actually speaking to us through our guilt and nothing is accomplished by hiding from it.

The fall of Camelot, brought about by the adultery of Lancelot and Guinevere, was necessary that Britain might enter "ordinary time". Every relationship has its own Camelot, splendid in proportion to the quality of the lovers' relationship. The rewards come, however, not at once, but only after "the dark night of the soul; after something of seemingly highest importance is destroyed; after our hearts are broken."

Haule describes another classical story of "transformation in love making" - the spiritual journey of Teresa of Avila. In her earlier years she enjoyed "a spiritual and somewhat bodily lovemaking with her confessors." From a literal point of view, writes Haule, this might appear grossly sinful, but in the context of her whole life it was clear "the Holy Spirit was leading her; for these human affairs were explicitly about the love of God". They nourished her mystical longings as she was led by them to "more and more subtle and sublime experiences of love".

LOVE AND REGRESSION

Being 'in love' may also be a compromise against 'letting go', even though the experience of being 'in love' may appear the most amazing out-pouring of self. The idealisation of a partner, so characteristic of being 'in love' reveals what the lover is searching for: the impossible hope of the inner Child of being loved entirely by its parents; of bathing in and returning the warmth of their entire approval; of satisfying infantile sexual phantasy; of returning to the breast or the womb. In an extra-marital affair, being 'in love' will also involve a rebellion against the Super-Ego/Ego alliance and may indeed be recognised consciously as such, especially where the established partner is seen as having reinforced that alliance. Freud described the state of being 'in love' as (11):

> a flowing over of ego-libido to the object. This state has the power to remove repressions and to restore perversions. It exalts the sexual object to the position of sexual ideal ... this stage results from the fulfilment of infantile conditions of love, we may say that whatever fulfils this condition of love becomes idealised.

If the idealised sexual relationship should fail us, infantile rage and despair arise into consciousness with enormous force. Sexual partners provide a ready object onto which to project this rage and despair. Just as all that is loved may be loved in the partner, so all that is hated may now be hated in the partner. As Sartre observes profoundly (12):

> hate is the hate of all Others in the Other ... the Other whom I hate actually represents all Others.

Eros may find sometimes a deflected form of expression through sexual relationships or sexual behaviour disapproved by the internalised Parents. The orientation of the sexual behaviour to its roots in childhood provides a concession towards regression on the part of the Ego and an actual rebellion against the Super-Ego/Ego alliance. This rebellion may, however, be denied at once so forcefully by the Ego that the sexual behaviour appears to consciousness as a compulsion. It appears sometimes, when witnessing the struggle of a client in this type of dilemma, as if Eros would actually go so far as to destroy us in order to find some expression, some movement towards the resolution of the dynamic ills standing in the way of its purposes.

As long ago as the fifties, in *The Art of Loving* (13), Erich Fromm was distinguishing neurotic and non-neurotic love. Usually, he wrote, when most of us claim to love someone else, we love them in a possessive manner, as if they were an owned object. We are not so much loving the person as what we want them to do for us. When a partner makes a bid for change this may be experienced as threatening one's control, undermining a sense of power or security. A growing trend in the divorce courts is separation over disputes attributed to the arrival of pets in the home, leading a partner to feel neglected and jealous. The choice of another sexual partner, sometimes heralding a failure in relationship, a bid for freedom, a disatisfaction with a schizoidal compromise, is often referred to as being 'unfaithful' to the marriage vow, whereas, of course, the core of the marriage vow (at least in secular and Nonconformist services) is not about sex at all, but about a commitment to a relationship for better or worse. 'Unfaithfulness' in this context belongs to the one who leaves the partnership because of a construed 'better' or 'worse', rather than stay and work it through to a new level of loving and caring. Spiritually speaking, unfaithfulness is the use of the marriage as a support, a container for the constructed selves of the partners, rather than as a vehicle for growth, maturation and freedom, (to the ends of *cupiditas* rather than *caritas*, as Augustine would have had it) within which the partners act as mirrors for one another and are prepared both for change and to be changed; accepting of the suffering change inevitably requires.

The sexual engagement of a partner with another person, the creation of a triangle, stimulates a regression to infantile experiences of loss, to the pain of early triangles with parents and siblings. We have lost the Breast and can no longer have it to ourselves. We are bereft of the phantasy of having at last found the solution to our inner emptiness and alienation by having found someone, we fondly believed and hoped, who would become Mother/Father to us and give us the unconditional holding we never possessed. This regressive pain, bringing us alarmingly close to the Abyss, triggers the negative face of our central or core transference and gives opportunity for hidden rage to arise and cathect to our partner as convenient object. Most people are not in any way equipped to see this angst, this heartache or heart break, as a spiritual or psychological opportunity to wean from a neurotic and dependent love to a mature and independent love; to work through trauma long unresolved in the unconscious. But most of us who have practised therapy will have worked with people for whom this kind of trial has indeed had a creative outcome; who were able to come to see the struggle and pain of the trauma of a partner's adultery as their personal 'karma' or as their 'guru', a means of transformation and maturation for both partners.

Luce Irigaray has suggested that the separation from the Breast is not the first traumatic experience of abandonment, but rather that the primary act of separation is the loss of the umbilical cord; of emerging into the world from the safe-inside experience of the womb. She considers the penis an umbilical phallus, inasmuch as it is a tube of flesh which joins two bodies. Through this umbilical phallus partners hope to find their way back into their Mother's body, seeking a long lost unity and sense of belonging. After orgasm some partners express the desire that the penis could remain within the vagina for ever; whereas others, as if in resentful despair of ever rediscovering such unity or in ambivalent anger against the anticipated end of coitus, remove/expel the penis quickly in a sudden return, as it were, to themselves. The regressed Ego, of course, desires to share neither the Breast nor the Umbilical Phallus. The investment partners place in their sexual engagement is related to the desire to lose one's self in the Other - an Other who will never face me with the trauma of separation, thus, hopefully, making the risk of self loss without danger. In this case coitus represents a desire, however unconscious, to return to the Womb with the hidden, but ultimate possibility of being born anew - allowing the reparative project of the regressive programme to pursue the promise offered in the concept of the Commonwealth of God.

A sustained and committed sexual relationship that persists after the being 'in love' phase has passed, may permit us to value a relationship that is not idealised. But we have to begin where we are, whether enjoying quiet compatibility or caught in the cat-and-dog life, the tit-for-tat scene of partners unable to see through their infantile projections. With struggle and heartache, with patience, forgiveness, humility, tolerance and good humour, the relationship may keep one foot in the realities of the life situation, whilst the other foot tests the waters of the regressive programme. A metanoia may occur that will fulfil the promise of the marriage ceremony, allowing the relationship to become a prototype for a deeper union, the spiritual and androgynous marriage in each partner of Eros and Psyche - of the soul with the psychobiological potentiality represented by the God archetype.

If people use their sexual relationships to help each other face the hidden pain of the soul rather than manipulate their partners to avoid that pain; if they sustain each other in depression rather than flee depression in search of superficial release in so-called happiness; if they speak and accept the truth in love and do not dissemble, examining who they are and how they have come to their present estate, the relationship will mature in ever-widening circles of understanding and inter-personal commitment. They will discover that grief is at the heart of all our joys and how joy nestles in the very womb of grieving.

Such relationships will permit that true letting go which brings us through the many trials of the regressive programme - including acting out - to inner harmony. Such relationships, forgiving of fault, respectful of human freedom and privacy and unbearing of grudge, will support each partner whilst s/he plumbs spiritual depths in search of the union described in Christian Doctrine as the hypostatical union of the soul with God. In this experience of union, the goal of the profoundest journey life has to offer, we discover with the saint that it is no longer we who love, but Love (*Agape*) that loveth through us. It is of the nature of that wholeness known as holiness that love is not confined to one or to a few idealised persons or objects, but flows out unconditionally into the whole world of people and things.

Sexual desire may be diverted in the most unpromising ways, towards objects as remote and even absurd as a boot in fetish. But diverted sexual desire is infinitely more desirable than none at all. Sexual desire draws us toward the resolution of the 'autistic pocket' through the erotic, whether the erotic is expressed in sexual/genital behaviour, in artistic creation or inter-personal relationships within the home or beyond it. The Ego/Super-Ego alliance attempts, however, to create a compromise by manipulating sexual desire in ways that maintain its own boundaries and defences. The work of Eros is thus impeded and diverted, setting up dangerous tensions and inner conflicts, which may eventually destroy the individual by undermining social and inter-personal relationships. In avoiding inner disturbance and anguish the Ego eventually creates outer chaos. If the inner chaos is tolerated, Eros will bring the person through to stability, increasing maturity and the realisation of lost potential, since Eros is the champion of our potentia - God in us.

Sexual desire, though perverted to excess (and perversions are clearly a bid for freedom arising from the Underworld, expressing counter-cultural rebellion - which is why they draw such bitter persecution), will nonetheless, with faith, love and understanding, turn like a tributary lost in marshy ground, back to the main stream and from there to the river and even to the sea. Sexual desire, however it may manifest itself, is the recognition of a movement towards a mystery - the mystery of the Other Person and the mystery of one's inner Self. All forms of sexual desire and expression, including those condemned (perhaps especially those condemned) by the community as deviant or perversion, represent a search - no matter how unconscious, misdirected or aborted - for one's own gender, identity and self-fulfilment. When the river meets the sea, sexual desire becomes a passion, a theophany - a passion for God.

NOTES ON CHAPTER TWO

1   Sartre, J.P. *Being and Nothingness.* Methuen. tr. Barnes, H.E. 1966 ed. Pp. 371 - 6

2   Sartre,J.P. Ibid. P. 626

3   Zaehner, R.C. *Concordant Discord.* Oxford. 1970. Pp. 164-171

4   Zolla, E. *The Androgyne.* Thames and Hudson. 1981. P. 72

5   Freud, S. *Collected Papers.* Hogarth. tr. Baines, C.M. 1957 ed. Pp. 30 - 59

6   Tustin, F. *Autism and Childhood Psychosis.* Hogarth. 1972.P. 62.

7   Tustin, F. Ibid. P. 87.

8   Psalm 46, v 10

9   Luke 9, v 24

10   Person, E.S. *Love and Fateful Encounters.* Bloomsbury. 1989. P. 341

11.   John R. Haule. *Divine Madness: Archetypes of Romantic Love.* Shambhala Pubs. 1990. Pp.   256/7 & 270/1.

12   Freud, S. Ibid. P. 41

13   Sartre, J.P. Ibid. P. 411

14   Erich Fromm. *The Art Of Loving.* Allen and Unwin. 1957. page 43

CHAPTER THREE

DEVIANCY AND ABUSE

The process of Maggie's gradual discovery of a capacity within herself to forgive her father was rather like the gestation of a child: conception could be said to have occurred when she began to confront the paradox of her love for her father and yet her sorrow, pain and anger at what had taken place between the two of them ...

'It is as though Christ embraces my suffering, the evil, the darkness and despair and transforms it - transforms the sordid mess into something beautiful, a hidden treasure beyond value and price. I don't altogether understand the process, but I know that it is happening and in the recognition of this awesome mystery, God becomes for me, yet again, a whole new experience.'

> *Hidden Treasure.(1)*
> Muriel Green and Anne Townsend

Transgression love, outlaw love, these are the notions that prevail in ordinary consciousness and literary texts as well; Denis de Rougemont in his Love in the Western World largely contributed toward imposing the concept in its strongest form: love is adulterous.

... Because it has merged with the superegotic practice of law, marriage - a historically and socially determined institution - is antinomic to love.

> *Tales of Love.* Julia Kristeva. (2)

Not even Khan's best friends have been able to find anything good to say about his last book, published in 1988, which this creative writer did not live long enough to regret he ever wrote. The reason for mentioning it here is because it led to his final expulsion from the British Psycho-Analytical Society. Not even the awareness of a new series of operations which had deprived him of his voice could protect him from the disbelief and outrage of his colleagues. My personal attempt to induce him to resign was met with polite disdain.

> *Obituary*
> A. Limentani (3)

A man cannot always be estimated by what he does. He may keep the law, and yet be worthless. He may break the law, and yet be fine. He may be bad, without ever doing anything bad. He may commit a sin against society, and yet realize through that sin his true perfection.

The Soul of Man Under Socialism
Oscar Wilde (4)

What road could I take now? How could I show my face in public, to be pointed at by every finger, derided by every tongue, a monstrous spectacle to all I met? I was also appalled to remember that according to the cruel letter of the Law, a eunuch is such an abomination to the Lord that men made eunuchs by the amputation or mutilation of their members are forbidden to enter a church as if they were stinking and unclean, and even animals in that state are rejected for sacrifice: 'No man whose testicles have been crushed or whose organ has been severed shall become a member of the assembly of the Lord'.

Historia Calamitatum
Peter Abelard (5)

Transsexual persons, in particular amongst those people referred to, however ineptly, as deviant in our society, create confusion in the minds of so-called 'normal' members of the community - whose struggles with gender are less intense, more secret and largely unconscious - since they appear quite 'sane' and are able to live adequate, socially-adapted lives. The notion of being trapped in a sexually inappropriate body is quite alien to most people; as is the desire of the transvestite to wear the clothes of the opposite sex, when the majority of us are at great pains to establish our gender precisely through dress. Transvestites also challenge sexually straight individuals by their ability to adapt, live creatively and, often, with especial flair. Ironically, the study of transsexuals and transvestites has brought enormous insight into some of the origins of gender identity in 'normal' - gender adapted - people and is helping us understand those problems of gender universally present amongst us.

In *Sex and Gender* Stoller (6) gives a fascinating account of male transvestism, defining adult male transvestism as "fetishistic, intermittent cross-dressing in a biologically normal man who does not question that he is a male - that is, the possessor of a penis." To date, he claims, there is "no acceptable evidence" in the vast majority of cases of transvestism of any genetic, constitutional, or biochemical abnormality. But the effect of relationships with parents during childhood, Stoller believes, is crucial.

One consistent factor in the aetiology of adult male transvestism is the mother's need "to feminize their little boys", deriving from strong envy of males and a desire, however unconscious, to damage her son. She does this by the occasional, but consistent humiliation of dressing him as a girl and expressing the wish he were a girl in revenge for her own sense of "blighted femininity". As Fenichel argued (7) the transvestite appears to be the product not only of his own defences, but also of his mother's unconscious wish (searching, perhaps, for a 'phallic woman').

The father of male transvestites, far from protecting his son, usually ignores his wife's periodic cross-dressing of the child. These fathers are silent, passive men, often withdrawn from their families. A common trigger of overt transvestism on the part of the boy is the acknowledgment by the father of his son's cross-dressing, punished by making the boy dress even more completely as a girl, thus conveying that the punishment is expected to have the opposite effect than that implied by the notion of punishment. Such fathers are not merely passively tolerant of the cross-dressing, but co-inspirators with the mother. Frequently, the father of the transvestite has been conspicuous by his absence - perhaps even through death or divorce.

Stoller believes castration anxieties are exacerbated by developing "feminine wishes" and the adult male transvestite handles this threat through the phantasy that if females are evidence of "a state of penislessness", the cause is not hopeless if there are women with penises. There could be no better proof of this than becoming one's self a 'phallic woman'.

The later choice of girl friends and wives is also a significant factor in the development of adult male transvestism. He usually manages to discover a woman in many ways similar to his mother, so triumphing over his original trauma by relating to a woman who treats him as his mother did, but with whom, nonetheless, he can have sexual relations. Mothers and mother-surrogates of transvestites accelerate and exaggerate what is a normal process of feminine identification in small boys. The result of this is a problem in gender identity. He is sure of his sex, that he is male, but unsure of his gender as masculine or feminine. In the act of cross-dressing and masturbating or exhibiting his penis to himself, say in a mirror, he at once faces the threat of his feminine desires whilst especially asserting his male sexuality through a reassuringly erect penis; he confirms that the state of being feminine is not permanent and that it cannot destroy him.

The researches of Stoller and his team led him to believe that whilst there were male transvestites and male transsexuals, among women there are female transsexuals but no female transvestites; since, when dressing as men, women do not make a fetish out of their clothing. Kaplan, however, records some exceptions amongst women, notably Vita Sackville-West (8).

Whilst some cases of female transsexualism tempted one towards the postulation of primary biological forces, the more patients he saw and the more detailed the information about them he gathered, the more Stoller became convinced, nonetheless, of "psychological forces" initiating and conditioning the transsexualism.

SEX AND GENDER

Sex and gender seem to common sense to be practically synonymous and inextricably bound together. However, we now see that it is useful to distinguish sex as biologically determined and gender as the product primarily of cultural training. Research has followed the suggestion in Freud's monumental works, *The Interpretation of Dreams* and *Three Essays On Sexuality*, that much of what we ordinarily describe as sexuality develops out of early life experience. Amongst so-called classical experiments was one concerning two children born with the genetically normal internal sex structure of females (gonadally and endocrinologically female), though possessing external penis and testes. By the time these children were five years old the one who was unequivocally believed to be a girl, believed herself, without doubt, that she was a girl; whereas the one believed to be a boy was convinced he was a boy. The gender behaviour of these children was determined not by their sex (biological facts), but by their postnatal experiences - a complex process beginning with the authoritative labelling of these children by their parents.

However, there are a number of cases of children who were apparently anatomically male or female, who were wrongly 'diagnosed' male or female, whose 'hidden' anatomy has affected their gender choice against the authority of the parents. Such cases, however, argues Stoller, are rare and are the exceptions which prove the rule. The higher mammals all show degrees of both masculine and feminine behaviour in any individual; there is no such thing as "an exclusively masculine or feminine mammal." (Bonobo chimpanzee, for example, of both sexes are bisexual and promiscuous in their behaviour and enjoy masturbation - self or mutual with either sex.) Gender can be taught, although the sex of the person is determined by biology. Even when individuals are reared in the gender opposite to their biological sex a clear-cut gender identity develops within the assigned sex unless someone questions it. Beyond the age of two and a half it becomes increasingly difficult or impossible for most people to change gender, despite certain rare exceptions.

The conviction that biological forces were the essential and determining factors in our sex and gender, led to decades of speculation regarding alleged gross chromosomal anomalies in perversion with gender abnormality. It was especially alleged this would be the case with homosexuals and transvestites. Research revealed that no such defects were demonstrable - particularly in the cases of homosexuals and transvestites.

We are moving ever closer, it seems, to the recognition of human beings as bisexual creatures, capable of making different choices or preferences (usually culturally determined) in the gender of their partners. It is said that the concept of 'homosexuality' did not occur to anyone before the nineteenth century. Perhaps the polarisation of 'homo' and 'hetero' will seem quite dated during the twenty first century. Bixsexuality acknowledges the possibility not only of continous monogamous relations between partners of the same or opposite sex, or of triangular relaionships, but introduces the possibility of a model of relating that recognises the validity of four (or more) alternatives; implying that through our sexual relationships we may explore not only our 'complement' but also the 'same'. This possibility was, perhaps, well anticipated in the famous remark of Freud to Fliess: "You are certainly right about bisexuality. I am also getting used to regarding every sexual act as one between four individuals."

PERVERSION

The word 'Perversion' refers to a move away from a considered or agreed 'norm'. Perversion is offensive to people who identify firmly with their mores in the same way that differing theological positions have been considered offensive (heretical), by those claiming to be orthodox (i.e. 'correct'); and in the same way that certain schools of psychodynamics have been ready to excommunicate members whose theoretical position and/or behaviour have offended against an agreed concensus - as in the cases of Jung, Lacan, Kahn and Iragaray among others. The word 'perversion' has other root meanings, including 'to overthrow', 'to turn round' or 'to overturn'. These hidden meanings in the word are reverberating powerfully amongst many therapists towards the close of the millenium, as we discover the positive value of perversion as an attempt to modify, balance and inform the status quo. Kahn, for example, had argued in the late seventies, in *Alienation In Perversions*(9), how acting out could provide the pervert with reparative and restorative possibilities; and how much there was to be learned from the psychic structure of perversions.

People react to so-called perversions with astonishing horror and cruel rejection, yet these deviancies are clearly a response to appalling handling in childhood which is endemic in society. Perverts are like the Mediaeval lepers, tolling their bell for everyone. In preparation for the asylum the lepers were marched backwards, bells ringing, into the church for their own funeral service. The words of Donne are especially apt: "Ask not for whom the bell tolls, it tolls for thee ... No-one is an island". Perversions arise to bear witness to the hidden, unconscious ills of the community - from which people are in fearful flight - and also offer insight towards the resolution of the issues they raise for all of us. The pervert becomes like the painted bird in the story of the boy who captured a bird in a wood and took it home and painted its feathers. When he returned it to the wood its own kind turned upon it because of the difference discovered in the coloured feathers. They tore the painted bird apart. Difference, deviance, perversion threaten the established Ego system and its sense of security in the presence of a shared uniformity, an agreed sense of what is 'normal' and, therefore, 'healthy', which holds us above the danger of regression towards the Abyss. We aptly describe deviance as 'abysmal', unconsciously recognising in our use of the term, where our fears derive.

All manner of deviance, of course, offends some people greatly - the deviance of politics, of colour, of race and religion - but none seems to exercise people's disgust and loathing so much as sexual deviance. At the same time we are obsessed with sex and gender - our popular magazines are made up largely of articles on sex and fashion (fashion as gender appearance), as a glance on the racks of any newsagent will confirm. The family unit is used not only as agent of political and economical control beyond our homes, we control it also ruthlessly from within in our terror of offending against the accepted heterosexual sterotypical caricatures of male and female, husband and wife, parents and children. In such a climate the difference of deviancy is so much to be valued.

Michel de Montaigne in his *Travel Journal* (10) tells of a girl who came to Vitry, where Montaigne was staying. She dressed as a man and worked as a weaver. The young woman so successfully carried off this convincing piece of transvestism that s/he fell in love with a woman and married her. They lived together for several months without complaint from his/her partner until s/he was recognised by someone from her home town in Chaumont-en-Bassigni. The young woman was forced to abandon her male clothing and was condemned to be hanged for her offence. She said she would rather be hung than return to a woman's status. And she was, indeed, as Montaigne puts it, hanged "for using illicit devices to supply her defect in sex." Similarly, Laqueur tells of a man who was burned at the stake in the late fifteenth century for living as a woman - "for flouting the conventions that make civilization possible"! (11).

HOMOSEXUALITY

One remembers more recently the fate of highly creative people such as Oscar Wilde, who spent two years in prison on charges of homosexual conduct presented by his partner's father; and Tchaikowski, who was intimidated into suicide rather than risk the reputation of the School of Jurisprudence should charges of homosexual behaviour be made public against him. In the case of Wilde, having raved about his *The Importance of Being Earnest*, the great British public indulged in one of its well known fits of hypocritical, holier-than-thou morality as this talented man's life was laid in ruins.

Although in some communities, such as the Greece of the time of Socrates, homosexual relationships were honoured and human bisexuality considered healthy and natural, in other cultures homosexuality has been fiercely and cruelly condemned. One cannot but assume that cultures condemning homosexuality are cultures where people are extemely unsure of their sense of gender and thus of their sense of identity. In Bahamian law, for example, where homosexuality is included in the sub-sections involving bestiality (!), the penalty for sexual intercourse in public by heterosexuals is a 150 dollar fine; whereas the same act between homosexuals, men or women, is twenty years in prison - which is three times the penalty for rape and four times the penalty for deliberately passing AIDS. It will come as no surprise to discover a blatantly patriarchal society, where women are subjugated and confined within stereotypical domestic roles. Homophobia represents a fearful and powerfully paranoid response to the threatened rise into consciousness of aspects of gender strongly repressed within the community, as dangerous to a fragile sense of coherence barely contained by long-established, traditional caricatures of gender roles and expectations.

Nowadays the psychodynamic and psychiatric literature is filled with references to the relationship between paranoia and the struggles of cients against their own latent, unacceptable homosexuality; a struggle intensified by social attitudes towards homosexuals, by homophobia. Stoller(12) suggests it is not, however, a satisfactory explanation to account for the paranoia by reference only to social disapproval, though it certainly must play an important role. Indeed, it would be surprising to hear an experienced therapist claim paranoia as a constant factor in the struggles of people with latent homosexuality, since latent homosexuality is always a gender issue (proceeding at least from our inherent bisexuality as human beings), eventually, in any therapy that goes to depth and it is certainly not always accompanied by a paranoia more severe than that commonly found amongst human beings; in addition most homosexuals manage to be so lacking in clinical paranoia, so very unpsychotic.

Stoller believes something much more profound than internalised social or parental disapproval threatens the person. He thinks the threat is not so much that of being homosexual as the threat that one will no longer be one's self; that is, the person feels s/he is losing her/his identity. Stoller is aware of the controversies over the use of the word 'identity', but believes that, although the word may be misused and is not adequately defined, it "still says more than if it were fragmented metapsychologically into structural parts." I also feel the term still has a valuable role to play in describing the relationship between the Ego-system and the Other. It is as if there are Ego-syntonic elements at the boundaries of the Ego system which, like the platelets of the body's immunity systems, somehow know what is 'me' and what is 'not me'. The immanence of 'not me' elements from the repressed 'areas' of the unconscious noises a grand alarm in the psyche comparable with, say, the reaction of the body to a virus - in fever, nausea and palpitations.

Clearly, as Stoller argues, homosexuals who are comfortable in their sense of identity, have chosen a gay gender role, and have learned how to live fruitfully and creatively in homosexual relationships, male or female, are by no means threatened by their homosexual identity, although they may suffer prejudice and even persecution in many societies. Their paranoia, such as it is, is reality based. On the other hand, people whose identity is firmly anchored in homosexuality may well be threatened by the emergence of their heterosexual feelings.

Massive indignation, joining the Moral Right (found, alas, on all sides of the political spectrum - left, right and centre), allows people to separate out from deviance and perversion. Knowing where the boundaries are and feeling sure of your own ability to remain within them gives enormous strength to frail Ego systems, bolstering them against any threat of regression to the Abyss. Clearly, to judge from the ferocity of people's response, nothing threatens them so deeply as sexual deviancy; which in turn indicates the enormous power of our sexuality as a revolutionary force in personal and social living. People impoverish their own spirit, inhibit the creative possibilities inherent in their own souls, by this dissociation, which inevitably leads to a schizoidal relationship with deviants and, one would thus expect, also with those closest to themselves. Personal and social freedom, religious and political freedom are intimately conjoined with sexual freedom.

THE WOMAN TAKEN IN ADULTERY

In *The Gospel of Thomas* (13) is the enigmatic statement: "Jesus said: The one who will know the Father and the Mother will be called 'the child of a prostitute'." Perhaps, the commentators suggest, this is a reference to *John* 8: 42, where some people say to Jesus "We were not born of fornication!" seeming to imply that Jesus was. They do not know God, but Jesus (child of fornication?) does. Taken simply at face value the text suggests that to know God requires some kind of intimacy with deviance, social unacceptedness, the Child of the left-hand path. Stained glass windows of Christ on the Cross frequently follow the Fourth Gospel's representation of the crucifixion scene by including three other dominant figures in the foreground or to one side - the mother of Jesus, Mary Magdalene and Saint John. The absence of the father of Jesus is startlingly obvious. It is usually assumed Joseph was dead, but if so the event is considered unworthy of note in the Gospels, whereas one cannot for a moment imagine that Mary's death would have passed unrecognised.

The four figures, however, have something significant in common - deviancy. Joseph, after all it would seem, was blameless before the Law; was there, perhaps, no place, therefore, for him here? They form, also, these figures, a quaternity of two men and two women - the number of integration, the number also of the number also of bisexuality, if we remember Freud's description of the unconscious bisexuality of partners as 'four in a bed'. What is it that integrates, then? Is deviancy (as an unconscious surge towards the hidden quaternity of bisexuality) the crucible of integration? To have been pregnant out of marriage Mary would have had to have been a prostitute. Her genealogy, of course, does point to a dark and hidden side of her nature - traced through Bathsheba, who committed adultery with David, Ruth who seduced Laban, and two prostitutes. Mary Magdalene, traditionally, is conceived as a prostitute and, perhaps, the mistress of Jesus. John, the disciple whom Jesus loved with a special love, is sometimes considered also the lover of a bisexual Jesus. What does this scene convey about a crucifixion of spirit (the body often looks stylised and unearthly, pale, without blood or pubic hair) which leads to an entombment (Abyss?) and a Resurrection - a restoration of spirit, a regeneration?

The Gospels continually reveal how the 'outrageous behaviour' of Jesus offended his contemporaries, often designated simply as ' the pharisees' and 'the scribes'. The 'religious' found his behaviour unacceptably deviant: his delight in feasting, for which they dubbed him 'wine bibber', 'drunkard and glutton' (charges he does not deny); his joy in living, which overflowed even on the solemn entry to Jerusalem amongst the Passover pilgrims; his speaking with the Samaritan woman; his healing on the Sabbath; his keeping company with tax gatherers, prostitutes and other 'sinners'; his ultimate blasphemy in maintaining silence before the High Priest.

If we apply Jung's theory of compensation to the vision of the Voice from Heaven at the baptism of Jesus, declaring: "this is my beloved son, with whom I am well pleased!", then we expect that the Primary Thought Processes make use of the extraordinarily forceful medium of a vision (a projected dream or phantasm of the day), rather than the more ordinary medium of a dream, because the content is far removed from surface consciousness, i.e. the Secondary Thought Processes. In other words, the message of the vision is quite unexpected by the conscious Ego and, perhaps, the opposite of what the Ego would have anticipated. It was certainly the last thing the good folk of Nazareth expected, the very town in which he had been reared: "Isn't this the carpenter's son?"

Everyone is God's beloved child, as Paul discovered on the Road to Damascus when, as he worked out his sadistic spleen in zealous persecution of the Christians, a Voice spoke to him, made a disclosure that shattered and transformed his life. Paul now knew, beyond all doubt, that Love was offered not because we had earned it through any merit of our own, through being 'good' (blameless within the Law), but as a free gift. His experience confirmed the wisdom in the ancient tag: "The greatest sinners make the greatest saints."

"I did not learn my theology all at once," wrote Luther, "but I had to search deeper for it, where my temptations took me ... A theologian is born by living, nay dying and being damned, not by thinking, reading or speculating."

Does our normally schizoidal horror against the deviant, whom we cannot see as a 'person', with whom we cannot identify but are, rather, at pains to distance ourselves, prevent us from realising regeneration in our own lives; whilst the identification with the deviancy unconsciously alive within us all, actually brings us to the crucifixion of spirit, which is the necessary prerequisite of holiness? As Schillebeeckx argued in *Jesus* (14): "salvation is given to people who in their sense of its opposite, of misery and evil, fulfil the only proper condition for eventually being able to receive the gospel as glad tidings."

One thinks of the story of the Buddhist King, Asoka, who asked his priests and councillors if they could make an Act of Truth to make the Ganges flow backwards. But no-one could. However, on the river bank stood an old prostitute, Bindumati, who performed her Act of Truth and the Ganges flowed backwards with a great roar. "How is it," asked the King, "that you, a thief and prostitute, a corrupt and wicked old sinner, can make the Ganges flow backwards?"

The woman replied: "Your Majesty, whosoever gives me money, be he a Ksatriya or a Brahman or a Vaisya or a Sudra, or of any caste whatsoever, I treat them all exactly alike. Free alike from fawning or contempt, I serve the owner of the money. This is the Act of Truth by which I caused the mighty Ganges to flow back upstream."

When the woman taken in adultery was brought before Jesus, the warm compassion of Jesus, who clearly is 'there' and sees her as a 'person', is starkly contrasted with the schizoidal behaviour of her accusers, whose sadistic condemnation of this deviant person does not allow them either to be 'there' or to see the woman as a person. Why is the man with whom she had committed adultery not brought forward also? There is no mention of him. The story is told only in John (in an appendix at the beginning of chapter eight) and is considered an interpolation, although it is an ancient story. Clearly the gospel editorial censors had great difficulty with it, revealing, perhaps, where their sympathies actually lay.

The woman is treated by everyone involved, except Jesus, as an object. No-one, except Jesus, speaks to her or allows her to speak. They 'caught her in the act'; they 'led her forward'; the hostile crowd distance themselves on their high moral ground (the Moral Right) from her as a deviant 'it'; the breaking of the legal, social contract is more significant to them than her 'human' life. There is no 'I-Thou' here, but only an 'I-It' relationship. Their sadism and cruel violence, hidden by the respectability of compliance, is revealed openly before Jesus and yet hidden behind their self-righteous complicity. Further it is a trap laid for Jesus, since if he does not condemn her he will violate Mosaic Law, and if he does condemn her he violates Roman law (at this time the power of the Sanhedrin to apply a death sentence was removed by Roman decree).

Jesus does not answer, but writes in the dirt (a mark, perhaps of his disgust with them?). They press for an answer and Jesus challenges them individually, spiritually, by suggesting they look into their own hearts: "Let the one who is without sin amongst you cast the first stone." Jesus is suggesting that adultery is only like any other sin, like simply thinking about committing adultery, let alone acting out the phantasy. Is there anyone without sin? Are we not all in the same boat? "Are we not all miserable sinners?" asks Dame Julian of Norwich: "Also God showed that sin shall be no shame to us, but worship."(15) She mentions great sinners such as David, Mary Magdalene and Paul in whom sin was "turned to them for worship". God does not blame us for sin, since, after all, "sin is no deed." Sin was the spiritual condition in which all human beings were trapped in this life, a condition from which God was pleased to restore us.

The crowd come to Jesus strong in their sense of self-righteous 'straightness', their sense of unity in conformity, bringing the woman pervert, the deviant one, from whom they distance themselves. Jesus reminds them of a different kind of unity, one they would rather forget; a unity which includes the woman, a unity of human frailty. His words press them also into another dimension. The sins that matter are not deeds, but the thoughts and phantasies of the mind, the spiritual condition of pride, revealed in the very self-righteousness with which they distance from the woman. Self-righteousness is more to be condemned than adultery. His words have impact on the crowd because he has managed to refer to a 'word-game', a shared field of reference, which, however obliterated by social prejudice, fear and inhuman passion, is still deeply embedded in their cultural heritage.

Adultery, as a perversion, represents the attempt to fill out existential emptiness, to bring presence into alienation. Those who bring the woman to Jesus are also empty and alienated and their schizoidal indifference to her as a person, reveals the extent of this alienation. In falling into adultery the woman has responded to the recognition of her alienation and its need of presence, whereas they who bring her to Jesus are still effectively maintaining their defences against the visage of alienation, by taking the high moral ground of the accuser.

Jesus is offering an old model of the casting out of evil, which had superseded - during the moral development of the Jewish people - the primitive and self-interested choice of a scapegoat; a model which sees virtue as developing out of the instant of self-recognition, a genuine discovery and acceptance of the sharedness of the 'guilty person's' existential situation with one's own. Jesus invites the people in the crowd to open themselves to their own lack of glory before God; to place themselves in the sinner's space as another human being fallen in the world, as they are fallen. Jesus is deconstructing polarised images, bringing hierarchically complemented concepts from the margins to the centre; always a dangerous enterprise and one for which he, like Socrates before him, would eventually give his life. He is disrupting the distinctions between the innocent and the guilty; the righteous and the sinner; the socially adapted person and the deviant; the 'good' murder of legal execution and the 'bad' murder of the deviant criminal.

ABELARD AND HELOISE

Amongst the more bizarre aspects of sexual deviancy are the regulations governing the sexual conduct of clergy down the ages. Whilst Augustine of Hippo was at Milan, for example, amongst the penalties for sexual misconduct was a thirty day fast for a priest caught masturbating in church - the penalty for a bishop caught masturbating was fifty days. The regulation clearly recognised that masturbating in church was a likely possibility! At different periods in the history of the church the regulations governing the sexual life of priests changed radically (though usually at the discretion of the bishop). Priests were able, for example, to take concubines, with whom they might have sexual intercourse, sometimes under the regulation of *coitus interruptus* and sometimes under the regulation of *coitus reservetatus* (the highest form of sexual engagement according to the *Kama Sutra*).

Writing to the Elector of Saxony concerning the sexual promiscuity of Landgrave Philip of Hesse, who had contracted syphilis, Martin Luther (16) revealed how he had hoped to contain the Landgrave's appetites by advising that:

> he might secretly keep an honest girl in a house .. and visit her from time to time, as great lords have often done. In like fashion I advised several clergymen under Duke George and the bishops secretly to marry their cooks.

Peter Abelard, born into minor Breton nobility in 1079, hailed as the greatest theologian of his time, fell in love with Heloise, whose guardian, her uncle Fulbert, was a canon in Paris. Begun as a calculating piece of seduction on his part, the relationship burst magnificently into a wild and passionate love affair in which Abelard was completely carried away, reckless in speech and behaviour, writing love songs sung by minstrels on the street corners - becoming the popular songs of the day.

Heloise became pregnant and Abelard moved her to Brittany, where their son was born and placed in the care of his sister. Abelard disguised Heloise as a nun and returned to Paris to make amends with Fulbert. He would marry Heloise so long as the marriage was kept secret. Heloise at first refused marriage, believing that if it became public knowledge her guardian would be enraged at the ensuing scandal and Abelard would be ruined. People would turn a blind eye if he kept her simply as his mistress, which was more acceptable than marriage in a clerical magister and scholar.

However, Abelard insisted and Heloise submitted to his will. He took her to the convent at Argenteuil and could not keep away, although his visits were disapproved by the authorities. Abelard declares how they were more persecuted now, after their marriage, than they had been before. Fulbert believed Abelard was trying to be rid of his niece by making her a nun and sent his servants in the night to the Paris hostel where Abelard was sleeping, with instructions to castrate him. And this they did. His screams brought students running too late. Abelard was now quite unable to relate sexually to his wife and lover. He became a monk and entered the Abbey of St. Denis.

His wounds were scarcely healed before the clergy called him to continue his teaching from the cloister. He became a spiritual director. Heloise was a nun until the end of her life, outliving him by many years. They turned the tortuous torrent of their passionate love towards God, but it was not easily done. In one of the many beautiful letters they exchanged(17), Heloise wrote:

> The pleasures of lovers which we have shared have been too sweet - they can never displease me, and scarcely be banished from my thoughts. Wherever I turn they are always there before my eyes, bringing with them awakened longings and fantasies which will not even let me sleep.

Concerning their marriage, she wrote:

> God is my witness that if Augustus, Emperor of the whole world, thought fit to honour me with marriage and conferred all the earth on me to possess for ever, it would be dearer and more honourable to me to be called not his Empress but your whore ... Who is there who was once my enemy, whether man or woman, who is not moved now by the compassion which is my due? Wholly guilty though I am, I am also, as

you know, wholly innocent. It is not the deed but the intention of the doer which makes the crime, and justice should weigh not what was done but the spirit in which it is done.

GALILEO

When people offered 'deviant' or 'heretical' models in theology they suffered the wrath of the Inquisition; merciless and brutal in the name of Christ. Giordano Bruno was burned alive in 1600 for supporting Copernicus, who in 1543 had announced the earth turns daily on its axis and revolves around the sun. This was only ten years before Galileo swung Old Discoverer on the skies. No wonder some professors refused to look through it. But many did and were convinced of the correctness of Copernicus' theories. Galileo found himself before the Inquisition (18). The heavenly movements he described were, they declared, contrary to scripture. Alternative views could not be tolerated; there was no room for difference (deviance).

Approaching seventy, infirm with a double hernia and palpitation of the heart, he faced the examining cardinals. He was threatened with torture unless he recanted his views. After four months detention he abjectly yielded to the Vatican, whilst still muttering under his breath: "Nevertheless, it does move." He was again imprisoned and his books placed on the Index of forbidden works, where they remained despite efforts by Catholic scholars, until 1835. Through the intercession of the Duke of Tuscany, Galileo was released to become a permanent prisoner in his own home, surrounded by spies, who nonetheless could not prevent scientists, philosophers and nobility from visiting, eager to see the gnarled features and piercing blue eyes of this chained eagle.

At risk of his life Galileo smuggled out bits of a new manuscript he was working on, feverishly for fear of failing sight, to circulate in countries where, he believed, the press was free. He died at 78 yrs of age in 1642, the year Isaac Newton was born. Even dead his memory inspired fear amongst his opponents, who tried to keep not only his works, but even his bones, hidden.

An Age of Faith was an Age requiring Certainty, not Faith; an Age in which Doubt was repressed. This is not Faith, but a parody of Faith. When doubt and uncertainty are repressed they become unconscious and therefore much more dangerous since they find terrifying and destructive ways of appearing in the world. In persecuting Galileo the priests were persecuting their own unconscious doubts and uncertainties. He represented uncertainty; his cosmology would have taken them along a tight-rope they dared not walk. As Hegel said of the Athenians who persecuted and killed Socrates: "It was a force within themselves that they were punishing."

EXCOMMUNICATION: LACAN AND KHAN

Inquisitions of one kind or another, with the power to excommunicate, imprison or destroy people, have been with us ever since. We recall the hysterical, ruthless witch hunts of McCarthyism in America and the unbelievable horrors of Stalin's use of the KGB and the atrocities of the gulags, made so vivid for us through the work of Solzhenitsyn (18).   But other, less powerful organisations, also have their 'Inquisitions' practising under the ruse of correct professional conduct (for the protection of the people!).   Persecution and excommunication seem endemic to the modernist cause; its desire to control and contain, to possess 'all truth' or believe in its possibility. It is especially sad when we see not only religious organisations such as the churches, but also great, humane and impressive movements like psychoanalysis practising exclusivity and the laying on of hands, preaching 'orthodoxy',   clinging to 'tradition' and 'scripture', exalting the word of revered founders and declaring deviant 'heresies' and 'heretics' anathema.

Jacques Lacan gave a paper in January, 1964, to an audience which included Levi-Strauss, at the Ecole pratique des Hautes Etudes on *Excommunication* (20). Lacan's teaching had been censured, he said, by "a body calling itself the Executive Committee of an organization calling itself the International Psycho-Analytical Association."   He had been told that the ban made on his teaching was crucial for his affiliation to that body and on the guarantee that his teaching "may never again be sanctioned by the Association".   Lacan asks what it is about that community "that is so reminiscent of religious practice"? Although it was no laughing matter, he declared, yet it was "material for comedy."

Another brilliant child of psychoanalysis, and a pupil of Lacan, Luce Irigaray, came before the psychoanalytical Inquisition and, in her own words, "was put into quarantine" by the psychoanalytical establishment after the publication of her outspoken views on feminism and psychoanalysis in her book *Speculum,* published in 1974.   One wonders what would have become of Heinz Kohut during the heated controversies over his elaboration of 'self psychology' had he not been president of the North American Psychoanalytic Association (21). Kohut blamed training analyses,   which had inadequately worked through narcissistic issues (e.g. narcissistic attachment to the role) , for the "excessive conservatism" and the "morality-tinged stance" some analysts took against perceived threats in theory and practice towards commonly held traditional ideas.

Lacan could take his excommunication light heartedly, since Parisian intellectuals gave him great support and a University post was created for him, but others, such as Ferenczi, found persecution undermining of health and vigour. In the Introduction to Ferenczi's *Clinical Diary* (22) Judith Dupont describes how Ferenczi's emphases on the hypocrisy of "certain professional attitudes of analysts" (such as the denial of countertransferential feelings they found uncomfortable or "contrary to their ethics", which he believed revived the very traumas in their patients' analysis was supposed to heal), brought heavy condemnation, the withdrawal of the facility for practising training analyses and even, in the case of Ernest Jones, untruthful representation of his mental condition (23). At his last interview with Freud, when he held out his hand, Freud, wrote Ferenczi, "turned his back on me and walked out of the room." Ferenczi was grief-stricken and bitter at Freud's behaviour, especially at his demand that Ferenczi should not publish work disapproved by Freud. Yet, to the end of his life, he remained loyal to Freud and psychoanalysis. As for Ferenczi's colleagues, writes Dupont, "they were protecting themselves from the unbearable upheaval that he advocated and initiated, by endeavouring to push him toward the pathological side" - out to the margins.

Psychoanalytical history, like religious history, is marred by the paradox that, frequently, psychoanalysts have been unable to tolerate the most brilliant exponents of the analytical art - such as Lacan, Jung, Ferenczi and, of course, Masud Khan. Frequently a core issue is that of the handling of transference and counter transference, the problem of intimacy as opposed to formality. It was obvious to Ferenczi, as it was to Jung and Lacan, that there was two-way traffic here; not only did the patient transfer disowned parts onto the therapist, but the therapist must also transfer disowned parts onto the patient. The claim that a training analysis would somehow produce a perfect therapist, incapable of such transference, or entirely detached from it was an impossible and unrealistic piece of grandiosity. It was as though Freud had invented a therapeutic model of relating as a refuge from intimacy - a space where intimacy could be studied without intimacy.

Ferenczi was determined to show Freud there was no conversation without either intimacy or the refusal of intimacy. How could two people go on sitting in a room together talking and continue to believe that one of them was more authoritative than the other? The recognition of the force of this argument led Jung to abandon the couch and free associative method and to sit, instead, face to face with the patient as an equal - as someone similarly struggling with the problems of being human; whose 'desire', to use Lacan's term, was equally significant to that of the patient. Here was a departure from the medical model of 'them and us'; someone who is 'healthy' helping someone who is 'sick' to become 'healthy' as the therapist is 'healthy'. One recalls that great and controversial therapist, Harry Guntrip, admitting how he was still, in his seventies, struggling with psychosomatic symptoms and their pathology relating to unassimilated trauma from infancy. Ferenczi was raising pertinent questions with Freud, such as: "Why would a person want to understand someone, or even cure them, rather than have sex with them? How could one protect a person's best interests by being unfriendly to them?" Psychoanalytic theory made these questions unavoidable, but Psychoanalytic institutions ruled them out of court.

Another great, eccentric and deviant child of psychoanalysis was Masud Khan, born in the Punjab in 1924, son of a Rajah owning a vast feudal estate. Judy Cooper, one of his analysands, in a personal tribute after his death in 1989 (24) wrote of his acute sensibility "which at once held a total and almost fatalistic tolerance and acceptance of any unusual behaviour." He had, she writes, an amazing ability to reach out and verbalize for others "the most unknowable parts of their experience and being. He could be compassionate beyond compare." In addition he had a brilliant and incisive mind.

Kahn's analytical technique was as unorthodox as his life. Often, apparently, he talked in session more than his patients, whilst "brilliantly exacting from them information essential to their treatment." Limentani, writing an obituary in *The International Journal of Psychoanalysis* (25), describes how 'the last straw' in his relationships with colleagues in the Association was when it was discovered he socialised with some of his patients (like Freud, of course, who not only analysed his daughter, but also the young couple, Mark and Ruth Brunswick, who frequented his home (26)). When it was believed Kahn had had sexual affairs with some of his analysands he was stripped of his role as supervisor of trainee analysts. Whilst he was seriously ill, having lost his voice from the latest series of operations, dying from cancer, such was the outrage of his colleagues over his latest book (27) they could not be restrained from pressing for his excommunication. An attempt by Limentani to induce him to resign "was met with polite disdain."

Kahn was a brilliant theorist as well as an excellent analyst (amongst his papers were discovered scores of letters from grateful patients) and wrote illuminating and original books included in the International Library of Psychoanalysis. He received analysis from Dr. Latif, an American psychoanalyst for three years. During his psychoanalytical training he received analyses from no less gifted therapists than Ella Sharpe, John Rickman and Donald Winnicott. The first two died during Khan's therapy, but his relationship with Winnicott, long and complex, spanned twenty five years until Winnicott's death in 1971. His clinical work was supervised by Melanie Klein and Anna Freud, who endeared herself to him by standing by him in mid career when an indiscretion led to the possibility of his being excommunicated then. Anna Freud had said that if he were excommunicated psychoanalysis would lose one of its most creative minds.

What more could one do to become the 'perfect' analyst, the completely integrated psychotherapist, than to undergo such prolonged training, therapy and supervision with the best analytical minds Britain could supply? No such person exists as the 'fully integrated therapist'. The concept is a piece of idealised grandiosity; an extension of the same kind of grandiosity which the Association has continuously maintained in its relations with those psychodynamic therapists who have not attended their Institute. Does the behaviour of the Association towards Kahn reveal the cool decision of balanced, integrated and mature minds or does it suggest minds more concerned with the respectable image and respectability of psychoanalysis and, therefore, with their own image and security than with a humane concern for a brilliant deviant, who had pushed forwards the boundaries of analytical theory and technique? Surely it was Kahn's very pathology which fed his developing insight and made possible his significant contribution to psychodynamic theory? The parallels between these incidents and the behaviour of dogmatic, esoterised religious fundamentalists towards those whose insights and behaviour does not conform to what is 'orthodox' and 'respectable' within their own interpretation of their traditions, with difference, is obvious, as Lacan was quick to remark.

In *Carnal Israel*, Daniel Boyarin (28) relates the Talmudic tale of the great Rabbi Abbaye, who became deeply depressed when he witnessed an unmarried man and unmarried woman take a long walk between villages without sexual encounter, since he knew he himself would have been unable to accompany the woman in such circumstances' without sex'. The very passion, he is informed by a wise old man, which drives him to study Torah would prevent him from simply saying goodbye. The desire is one and the only way he may keep himself from sin is by staying out of its way. The same drive that in the study house leads him to study Torah with such commitment is the very same drive, in the view of a certain left-handed Rabbinism, comments Boyarin, which will lead him into sin in such circumstances. The passion is one.

CARL GUSTAV JUNG - ADULTERY AND SEXUAL ABUSE

Early in his career, at about the time of his first meeting with Freud, Jung had a taste of the dangers of powerful positive transference and counter-transference in his work with a gifted young Russian Jew, Sabina Spielrein, who wished to have a child by him. Jung had a son at this time by his wife, Emma, and was so unsettled by Spielrein's response he tried to break the relationship. She attacked him, drew blood and left him, eventually writing to Freud about her predicament. Freud and Jung exchanged correspondence over this relationship and Jung made a confession of 'everything except intercourse' - according to John Kerr's account of the affair in *A Most Dangerous Method* (29). Freud responded that "to be slandered and scorched by the love with which we operate - such are the perils of our trade." Spielrein married a Jewish physician and went on to have a long and distinguished career as a psychoanalyst. Tragically, she and her two daughters were shot by the Nazis in 1941.

Jung's personal struggle with anima/animus projections did not, as one would expect, end here. Carl and Emma Jung had five children in the first eleven years of their marriage. Spielrein's letters to Freud preceded the birth of Emma's fourth child and so did the advent of Toni Wolff, a patient who became Jung's mistress. The presence of 'another woman', writes Maggy Anthony in *The Valkyries: The Women Around Jung* (30), was not unusual at that time in a 'conventional marriage'. What was unusual was that the three members of the triangle acknowledged the menage a trois and did their best to live with it, which they appear to have done successfully until Toni Wolff died in 1953, despite the great conflict and pain they each endured.

Emma engaged in analytical work, receiving one of her first patients from her husband's clientele, setting a persistent pattern, where many clients would have therapy with at least two of them. People who knew them during these years say, according to Anthony, that Emma seemed like a fulfilled woman who enjoyed her life and career. Jung told Freud he suffered from the 'nuptial conplex' and that "The prerequisite for a good marriage, it seems to me is the license to be unfaithful ... I think the French have found the solution in the Number Three. Frequently this number occurs in magic marriages." Anthony believes this was true of the Jungs' marriage.

It was to Toni Wolff Jung turned increasingly as he began his descent into his unconscious. Emma was, it seemed, the rock or foundation from which he felt secure to make this descent. After Toni's death Emma said: "I shall always be grateful to her for doing for my husband what I or anyone else could not have done at a most critical time." Whatever the agonies suffered by Carl and Emma, writes Anthony, the complications must have been worse for Toni Wolff. Whilst in some European countries there has always been a niche, however narrow, for the unmarried woman, no such niche existed in Swiss culture, where there was a law against 'adulterous meetings' and women have received the vote only in the second half of this century. Wolff had considerable literary gifts and wrote fine poetry. She became president of the Zurich Psychological Club and contributed intellectually through her writings to Jungian theory. Jung believed it was primarily through these struggles and conflicts he learned to understand the mysteries of the integrative path and the vagaries of anima/animus projections.

The ultimate goal of Jungian analysis, or the process of individuation, writes Anthony (31), is the *hieros gamos*, a term borrowed by Jung from mediaeval alchemy. His last great work *The Mysterium Coniunctionis* was devoted to this theme. She believes the women around Jung (including also Jolande Jacobi, Hilde Kirsch, Esther Harding and others) used their relationship with him to act out the *hieros gamos*, feeling 'married' to him at a deep level:

> the life-sustaining nature of the deep union is shown in the long, productive lives of these women. In each case, their relationship with Jung enabled them to live their lives at a very deep level, and their dreams and visions sustained them beyond the death of the man who had taken them seriously for the first time.

If therapists of the enormous stature of Jung find themselves compulsively acting out in therapy, committing both adultery and sexual abuse, it is suprising we do not encounter a great deal more of this kind of acting out amongst therapists at large. My experience of working with therapists, men and women (for women, also, offend, though less frequently it seems, against these psychotherapeutic mores), suggests to me that such acting out is a Razor's Edge - down one side lie creative possibilities and down the other dreadful destruction. A significant factor in the outcome of such relationships lies, as it does in other kinds of deviance and abuse, in the way in which people work at the implications of their own behaviour in a mutual attempt to understand and work through their pathology.

It is unrealistic to expect that therapeutic training alone will protect therapists and their clients from these trials of the Left Hand Path. It is not that the rules of therapy, the codes of conduct, are not good sense and well founded. Clearly they are, but the Law, whilst good, is a servant and not a tyrant, otherwise the Law will 'kill'. When one of the large Nonconformist traditions was informed, after a survey by sociologists, that sexual deviance and abuse was higher, statistically, amongst their clergy than amongst the rest of the population, the Synod reacted by asserting they would look more closely into selection procedures. It would surely have been more fruitful to enquire why the ministry attracted men and women who acted out in these ways - to have reflected on the relationship between deviancy and spiritual vocation; that is, the search for Love.

Instead of using the ruthless alternative of excommunication it would be more in line with the compassion expected of churches and therapeutic organisations alike if they had some system whereby offenders could be held - a category of temporary suspension perhaps - whilst they pursued their own therapy and were given time and opportunity to work through the pathology behind their behaviour, allowing the possibility, on appeal, eventually to return to full status; respecting the conviction that people can change, can grow and mature.

Peter Rutter in *Sex In The Forbidden Zone* (32) found sexual abuse much more common than he had expected in what he calls 'The Forbidden Zone' - amongst doctors, psychotherapists, clergy, lawyers, teachers and workplace mentors. Those who have sex (considerably more men than women - since men are so much more frequently in power situations with women than women are with men) with their clients, patients, parishioners and students are usually not obviously disturbed people, but accomplished professionals, admired community leaders and respectably married. Sexual violation of trust is an epidemic, mainstream problem. The damage people cause themselves when they violate the boundaries of caring relationships is often elusive, because they are able to convince themselves they are satisfying a deep need in themselves as well, perhaps, as in their 'partner'. Yet in this mode of acting out, writes Rutter, they are abandoning "the search for aliveness" within themselves and are left "with more emptiness than before" in the denial of their psychic wounds.

Here is the crux of the matter. Clearly acting out is not to be encouraged or recommended. But the intimacy of a long-term involvement may bring to the surface of both people unresolved psychological issues pressing with such power from the unconscious that acting out may become compulsive. Of course there are guide lines for this situation. In the case of therapy, another therapist should be found (though this may be as traumatic and as counter-productive as taking children from their homes on discovery of abuse) or a long interval, say twelve months, be introduced between sessions. This is cool, sensible advice and procedure. But people caught up in passionate acting out often appear quite unable to behave in sensible ways. And sometimes, as I have seen in my own experience of therapy with men and women in this predicament, if they do not ignore the motivation behind their involvement and hold one another in the pain and conflict, and work at the resolution of their own pathology, such relationships can, indeed, have a creative outcome.

In my experience it is short-term sexual relations between therapists and clients, guiltily broken off, without possibility of working through the issues arising from the acting out of the transference, the yearning for a breast, the unresolved dynamics of relationships with parents and so on, which leave most damage behind. Where there has been no chance of reparation or reconciliation, no opportunity for the expression of anger, hurt and indignation, no space for exploring the existenz from which the acting out arose on the part of both therapist and client, it is unlikely the sexual engagement will be able to work through fruitfully. But where such opportunities are afforded the relationship can work through to a natural and mutual end of the sexual acting out to a new stage of relating within the transference, revealing the fruits of maturation on both sides - to a deeper, enriching understanding of their pathologies. After all, even when inappropriate, it is possible, in some circumstances, for the sex act to be a beautiful and nurturing experience, a special gift between the partners.

THE EROTIZED TRANSFERENCE

Transference love is part of the regression brought about by the therapeutic situation. Love is frequently evoked in other types of regressive situation: patients hospitalised for organic conditions frequently fall in love with their nurses, as do pupils with teachers and secretaries with their employers. These figures recapitulate the parent-child relationship. As Bergmann wrote in *The Anatomy of Loving* (33), when the original relationship to a parent leaves a residue of unhappiness and trauma, a powerful wish will emerge that the lover, in whatever guise, should heal the wounds. Symbiotic wishes are thus reawakened in a desire for unity, but with this also arises the fear of the engulfing mother. The turbulence in many love relationships, in and out of therapy, lies in this dynamic.

At a symposium on erotized acting out, organised by psychoanalysts, Bergmann ventured to suggest the acting-out therapist deserved their understanding as much as their condemnation, only to find himself entirely alone in his point of view. It was as if the profession needed a powerful collective defense against this temptation. And yet many analysts find they are brought, in their work with clients, to layers of their unconscious not dealt with in their own self-analysis. Inevitably this will be the case since analysis is a life-long process of growth and development for client and therapist alike. A highly erotized transference may occur at a vulnerable time in a therapist's life, when s/he is especially susceptible to respond with an erotized counter-transference.

Whilst recognising the creative possibilities inherent in working through an erotized transference and counter-transference therapists must of course, nonetheless, be alive to the dangers. An erotized transference may be the last-ditch stand against serious depression or an imminent psychotic episode. Since at the core both of erotized transferences in clients and erotized counter-transference in therapists often lies a history of incestuous relationships, infantile seduction and child abuse, therapist and client are stepping into a minefield. So much depends here on the personality resources of the 'therapeutic partners', the overall nature of their psychopathology and the quality of the relationship between them. A poor prognosis is not always the rule. An erotized transference is especially valuable for schizoidal clients, for whom it may provide the first contact with deep feelings; and it may be a useful introduction to a recognition of intense symbiotic needs.

The analysis of transference and counter transference are at the very heart of psychodynamic therapy as a means of preserving the sanctity of the 'other', the client, by analysing out ego-centred or ego/super ego liaison strategies that affirm the ego's desires and defences - so that the 'Other', the Self, may find expression. Transferential and counter-transferential analysis are ways of protecting the authenticity of the therapeutic encounter. In religious terms it is a way of recognising the client as 'alterity', as 'other' in a sacred sense, inasmuch as the Christa/the Buddha indwells the client as well as the therapist. "Where two or three are gathered together in my name," said Jesus, "there am I in the midst of them" (Mt.18:20). From ancient times - for example in the beautiful 'sitting-down-together-teachings', the Upanishads of the Hindu faith - people have practised this intimate form of self-exploration, where two people sit together, in the presence of the Third, in reverent respect of one another's individuality and potential. Clearly sexual abuse is an offence against this kind of relationship (of psychotherapy - i.e., literally, 'care for the soul'). But with humility, honesty and with love, even abuse can be transformed within the life of the Spirit; where Eros may lead us, however circuitously, into Agape. Immediately after the declaration by Jesus that he will be with two or three gathered in his name, Peter asks how often shall we forgive those who offend against us. "As many as seven?" he asks, as was required by the Law. "I do not say to you seven times," answers Jesus, "but seventy times seven."

HIDDEN TREASURES

Any therapist who has worked with victims of child abuse will want to support enterprises designed to protect children. But even here more harm may arise out of moral indignation and condemnation than out of serious attempts to understand the predicament, the existenz, of both abuser and abused. People want to push horrific experiences of abuse into unconsciousness. At first people in therapy, who have been sexually abused as children, may wish their memories would remain buried. They may be unable to understand and therefore quite unable to forgive the dreadful things that have happened to them. Survivors of sexual abuse carry scars into adult life still souring their patterns of relating and behaving.

Understanding what has happened, feeling into the background of abuse, does not mean forgetting or belittling what has happened, and should reach further than mere acceptance of the past. In *Hidden Treasures* (34) Green and Townsend write that they see 'coming to terms with abuse' as being about "journeying towards self-knowledge, self-worth, and seeking the freedom to love and be loved"; a journey "of growth and spiritual healing and of becoming increasingly whole".

I worked with a woman who came to believe the only intimacy she had known in childhood was an inappropriate intimacy with her father; and she recognised the same was true for him. It is undoubtedly the case, when a person relinquishes their sexual agenda towards their child or client, that relinquishment carries healing potentiality, saving the vulnerable one from injury. It is also true that recognising the vulnerability of the abuser may have healing power, especially if that recognition is mutual. From hating and despising her father the woman worked through to an understanding of his overpowering needs and compulsive acting out, assimilated her own anger, grief and indignation to the point where she could begin to relate anew to her father, with love and compassion for them both.

The recollection of abuse is always a screen memory, and, therefore, however horrific, reveals/hides the even more horrific existenz, spiritual milieu, of the child out of which the abuse has arisen. To this extent, whatever Freud's errors in failing to recognise the overt reality of sexual abuse in childhood, he was, nonetheless, therapeutically sound to see that the working through of the implications of the abuse lay in the analysis of the relationships of the child with the caretakers of infancy. The mental or spiritual milieu out of which the particular acts of abuse arise, is more damaging, that is, than the actual physical abuse itself, which so captures people's imagination and to which they react with rage and indignation. But hate and anger, however understandable, must be worked through; since they, too, belong to the defences holding the adult above the Abyss. Anger, murderous rage, certainly needs acknowledgment and expression in consciousness, but it may also be used as a continuous and persistent barrier against deeper understanding and the possibility of forgiveness, which threaten a return, albeit of enormous therapeutic potential, back to lost and abysmal existenz.

PERVERSION AND THE UNIVERSAL LAW

At the root of the word 'pervert', so often used as a vitriolic label separating someone aside from the human race, is (as we noted above) the meaning 'turned from the right way', but also 'to overthrow' and 'to subvert'. Janine Chasseguet-Smirgel in *Perversion and the Universal Law* (35) considers perversion is one of the essential ways and means we apply to push forward the frontiers of what is possible and to unsettle reality. She sees perversions not merely as disorders of a sexual nature affecting a relatively small number of people, but as a "dimension of the human psyche in general"; indicative of a 'perverse core' latent in us all. Perversions are attempts to subvert the Law and their aim is regression towards 'primordial confusion', towards a chaos, "the state of unity without differentiation that preceded the Creation". They are a bid, however misdirected and aborted, for freedom, a reconstruction or acting out of an infantile neurosis (36).

In our horror of the perversions, the intuition that they are leading to the Abyss, in the desire to distance ourselves from the difference of deviance, we see the 'other', the pervert as someone with an irresistible attraction towards some abnormal or bizarre sexual behaviour. What, however, distinguishes perversion is not its bizarre or deviant appearance, so much as "its quality of desperation and fixity"(37). As Louise Kaplan writes perceptively in *Female Perversions:* "A perversion is performed by a person who has no other choices, a person who would otherwise be overwhelmed by anxieties or depression or psychosis." It is an appeasement of personal demons.

We are led astray, Kaplan writes, by the 'official' definitions of perversion, from the recognition that the so-called perversions are primarily pathologies of gender role identity, so that, in fact, "socially normalized gender stereotypes are the crucibles of perversion." It is as if the person we call 'pervert' has crossed a line, which makes visible what is present, but invisible in everyone; makes evident in his/her overt behaviour what is hidden and even denied by the community; makes observable what is covert in society. The rage and indignation against the 'pervert', like that against any 'deviant', is that the pervert has, by bringing out into the open what is unconscious/hidden in one's self, endangered the internal relationship of the Ego to the Shadow or repressed aspects of our mental life; so that aspects of ourselves incompatible with the Ego Ideal, which we fear will make us unacceptable to others and the Other and lead to our abandonment and regression towards the Abyss, are now threateningly closer to the surface of our own minds through the pervert's behaviour. The Super Ego, in internalised Parent mode, makes a virulent effort to retain the status quo through overt expressions of rage and condemnation and a reaffirmation of the received mores.

One of the most derided, but least damaging, of perversions, voyeurism, is clearly commonly found amongst us and accounts for the undying popularity of pornographic magazines and videos. But even a most serious form of perversion, such as the sexual abuse of children by their parents, where a parent has used a child both to experience intimacy and to express anger, appears as an acting out (in a manner that it is difficult/impossible to ignore simply because of its evident pathology) of the common/hidden tendency of parents to seduce their children through the imposition of received and unquestioned value systems of dubious quality, to use children to realise unfulfilled phantasies of significance and belonging; to expect that children will provide lost parental hopes of someone who will love me completely and whom I may love completely; to blame and harrass children when they cannot provide the nourishment we need and so on and on. The lengths to which some people will go to have children and the deep trauma they express at their childlessness reveals something of the enormous investment people put into the role of parenthood and the great expectations they hold for the contribution their children will make to their own, that is to the parents' lives. Such investment inevitably maintains an existential and covert violence of which the overt violation of people is a symptom, revealing what is otherwise hidden - off-scene.

Studies of cases of non-accidental injury revealed how common was the feeling on the part of the abusing parent that the child had seriously let them down, caused devastating hurt and disappointment, by not meeting the unrealistic phantasy needs of that parent. Parental rage against the child was an expression of infantile rage against their own treatment or handling when they were small children; the infant's inability to meet parental needs produced a regression in the parent to their own unassimilated infantile rage. A crucial factor in providing safety for these infants was, in fact, not to remove the child but to provide someone who would 'mother' the abusing parent. Inevitably, we discovered, the abusers had been themselves overtly abused in infancy.

The pervert is caught in a dreadful, inhibiting, destructive prison, the product of overt or covert abuse in infancy, which they are 'acting out' in adult life; that prison, however, reflects, reveals and represents symbolically, the hidden prison-houses of the mind which the imposition of culturally conditioned gender stereotypes and patriarchal values and ways of relating, creates (and hides) in us all. In the pervert an urgent, overwhelming pathology presses what is otherwise hidden into an 'acting out', a breaking open in some of us from time to time, in desperate, compulsive attempts - usually futile and fruitless and sometimes horrifically destructive - either to fill or to protest against the dread emptiness within our souls, without losing the safety of the prison, the container that holds us above the Abyss.

However, confrontation with that pathology and a courageous attempt to absorb the emptiness lying behind it, may provide the pervert and his/her victims with a genuine possibility of breaking out into something quite rare: to, on the one hand, an open, guilt free and frank recognition within one's self of the inhibitions and perversions of sexual and gender integrity, commonly hidden for us all (by the distorting stereotypes of sex and gender accepted and defined as normal and respectable within our communities); and, on the other hand a significant gain in possibilities for genuine reciprocal intimacy, a new capacity to live creatively with suffering - fear and despair - and a freeing of the imagination. The deviancies and the perversions offer us a challenge, a new possibility of rediscovering lost innocence; of knowing *'jouissance'* (with its hidden sexual connotation of *jouir* - 'to come').

NOTES TO CHAPTER THREE

1. Muriel Green and Anne Townsend. *Hidden Treasure*. Darton, Longman and Todd. 1994. Pp. 81 and 120.

2. Julia Kristeva. *Tales Of Love*. Columbia. 1987. P. 209. Copyright (c) 1987 by Columbia University Press. Reprinted with permission of the publisher.

3. A. Limentani. *Obituary.* Int. Journal Psych-analysis. 1992. 73, 155.

4. *The Works Of Oscar Wilde.* ed. John Gilbert. 1977. Cassell. Cf. also fm. Ballad In Reading Gaol:

The Chaplain would not kneel to pray
By his dishonoured grave:
Nor mark it with that blessed Cross
That Christ for sinners gave,
Because the man was one of those
Whom Christ came down to save ...

And all men kill the thing they love,
By all let this be heard,
Some do it with a bitter look,
Some with a flattering word,
The coward does it with a kiss,
The brave man with a sword!

5. *The Letters of Abelard And Heloise.* tr. Betty Radice. Penguin. 1975. P.76.

6. Robert J. Stoller. *Sex and Gender.* Karnac Books. 1984 ed. Pp.176 ff.

7. O. Fenichel *The Psychology of Transvestism* in Collected Papers, I, 167 - 180. W.W. Norton.   1953.
8.   Stoller. Ibid. P. 205 and Louise J. Kaplan. *Female Perversions.* Penguin. 1991. Pp. 237 - 241.

9.   M. Masud R. Khan. *Alienation in Perversions.* Karnac.1989 ed.Pp.28/9.

10.   Michel de Montaigne. *Travel Journal.* tr. Donald Frame. North Point Press. 1983. Pp.5-6.
11.   Thomas Laqueur. *Making Sex.* Harvard. 1990. P.138.

12.   Stoller Ibid. Pp. 154 ff.

13.   *Gospel Of Thomas.* Robert M. Grant and David Noel Freedman. Fontana Books. 1960. P. 180.

14.   Edward Schillebeeckx. *Jesus.* Collins. 1979. P. 197.

15. Dame Julian of Norwich. *Revelations of Divine Love. Burns* Oates.1952 ed. Pp.23,48,66.

16. Martin Luther. *Letters Of Spiritual Counsel.* ed. Theodore G. Tappert. SCM. 1955. P.290.

17. *The Letters of Abelard and Heloise.* tr. Betty Radice. Penguin. 1975. Pp. 114/5

18. Mario Biagioli. *Galileo,* Courtier. Chicago. 1994.
19. Alexander Solzhenitsyn.*The Gulag Archipelago.* Fontana.1974.

20. Jacques Lacan. *The Four Fundamental Concepts of Psycho-analysis.* Penguin. 1977. P.1 ff.

21. Luce Irigaray. *The Irigaray Reader.* ed. Whitford, M. Blackwell.1994 ed. Kohut, H. How Does Analysis Cure? Chicago. 1984. Pp. 160 ff.

22. *The Clinical Diary of Sandor Ferenczi.* ed. Judith Dupont. tr. Michael Balint and Nicola Zarday Jackson. Harvard. 1988. Pp. xvi ff.

23. See Paul Roazen. *Freud And His Followers.* Penguin. 1979. Pp. 358/9 and 368.

24. Judy Cooper. *Masud Khan: A Personal Tribute.* Free Associations. (1991) Vol.2, Part 1 (Number 21): 91-98.

25. A. Limentani. *Obituary.* Int. J. Psycho-Anal. (1992) 73, 155.

26. Paul Roazen. *Freud and His Followers.* Ibid. Pp.418/9.

27. M.Masud R.Khan. *When Spring Comes* Chatto & Windus. 1988.

28. Boyarin, D. *Carnal Israel,* California Univ. Press. 1993. Pp.62-65

29. John Kerr. *A Most Dangerous Method:* The Story of Jung, Freud and Sabina Spielrein. Sinclair-Stevenson. 1944.

30. Maggy Anthony. *The Valkyries: The Women Around Jung.* Element Books. 1990. P.15 ff.

31.   Maggy Anthony. Ibid. Pp. 109-110.

32.   Peter Rutter. *Sex In The Forbidden Zone*. Mandala. 1990. Pp. 1-2.

33.   Martin S. Bergmann. *Anatomy of Loving*. Columbia. 1987. Ch. 18.

34.   Green and Townsend. Ibid. Pp. 49 ff.

35.   Janine Chasseguet-Smirgel.*Perversion and the Universal Law* fm.
        Dimensions of Psychoanalysis. ed. Joseph Sandler. Karnac Books.1989.
        Pp. 177 ff.

36.   M.Masud R. Khan. *Alienation in Perversions*. Karnac. 1989. P.20.

37.   Louise J. Kaplan. *Female Perversions*. Penguin 1991. Pp. 10-15.
        page 71

CHAPTER FOUR

THE HOLY FAMILY:

ICONS AND IDOLS

Then let us traverse with daring
That predestined God-drawn ring,
From the Nothing to the All,
From the Cradle to the Bier,
Therefore let us risk our all ...
Acting and Desiring.

Karl Marx
Collected Works (I, 525-6)

Radical politics tend towards the same kind of political positivities and 'final solutions' as the 'conservative' regimes they purport to resist, transform, subvert or replace, with their categorical assertions of competing imperatives, identities and ends. (The identities and ends of 'women', 'blacks', 'minorities' or 'gays' for example.) Would-be radical politics thereby collude with the powers that be and bind us all the more securely to our assigned identities and political destinies (as woman, black or gay) by obscuring once again that experience of excess - of the space between reality and representation, being and being-as - from which they can be deconstructed and resisted.

Geraldine Finn
The Politics of Spirituality

It is a fact that the lover desires his or her passion to be legal. The reason may be that the law, which is external to the subject, is an area of power and attraction that can merge with the Ego Ideal. Nevertheless, once instituted for the subject, the law reveals its no longer ideal but tyrannical facet, woven with daily constraints and consonant hence repressive stereotypes ... Because it has merged with the superegotic practice of law, marriage - a historically and socially determined institution - is antinomic to love.

Julia Kristeva
Tales of Love

"You know perfectly well," says Mama Elena to her daughter, Tita, in Laura Esquirol's delightful novel of Mexican family life, *Like Water For Chocolate*, "that being the youngest daughter means you have to take care of me until the day I die." Tita, for the first time in her life, intends to protest against her mother's ruling.

"But in my opinion - "

"You don't have an opinion, and that's all I want to hear about it. For generations, not a single person in my family has ever questioned this tradition, and no daughter of mine is going to be the one to start."

Tita asked herself who had started this family tradition? If Tita couldn't marry and have children, who would take care of Tita when she was old? And what about a woman who marries and can't have children, who will take care of her? Typically, the women spent their lives in the kitchen, where Mama ruled with an authority beyond rebellion, passing on a well-established tradition that included every aspect of their lives, even down to sewing and basting clothes and the proportions of food in every recipe. The very word 'Mama' had a slightly disrespectful tone and the children were taught from infancy to use the word 'Mami' with a certain careful inflection.

Nonetheless, when her mother died, Tita wept genuine tears:

Not for the castrating mother who had repressed Tita her entire life, but for the person who had lived a frustrated love (1).

Tita swore in front of Mama Elena's tomb that, come what may, she would never renounce her own love.

Countless generations of women had passed on this tradition, so damaging to their own sex, unless someone, like Tita, had the courage and the independance to stand against it. Nothing, perhaps, inflames the wrath of some feminists more than the collusion of women in their own subjugation. Men, they will say, naturally because they are men, will ignore the subjugation of women, since it is apparently, however misguidedly, in their own interests; but how can women share in the perpetuation of their own bondage?

Tita knew that her own freedom to rebel, however constrained, arose out of the power and passion of her love. Love gave her the strength and the motivation to rebel. Love also allowed her to see the tragedy of her mother's life, lived in the dry and hollow frustration of an unrequited love. She recognised how her mother's role as Head of the Kitchen, She Who Must Be Obeyed, compensated for a profound inner sense of worthlessness, gave covert expression to a consuming indignation against her own life history and brought meaning and some shred of dignity into what, otherwise, appeared an undervalued and servile relationship with the men of the family.

Men and women have, from the beginning of recorded history, colluded in supporting stereotypical relationships, domestic prisons, damaging to them both, from which women might escape only by becoming witches, priests or prostitutes. Some women, especially of noble birth, could sometimes aspire to positions of great social significance. Pharoah Hatshepsut of the Eighteenth Dynasty (1567 - 1320 B.C.), for example, appointed his Queen to the religious office of second High Priest to the god Amon at Karnak (2). But even this appointment was, clearly, possible only through male patronage. Most women, throughout history, have been forced by cultural mores, supported by men and women alike, into a subservient, domestic role from which their sense of worth depended upon marriage - that is the woman's role as wife and mother. Matriarchy, the domination of a culture by its women, appears, so far as documented history is concerned, a concept invented by nineteenth century anthropologists such as Bachofen and Frazer. As Michelle Perrot and Georges Duby declare in their *A History of Women* (3), "in societies accessible to historical inquiry we find no trace of it."

George Frankl, however, in *Archaeology of the Mind* (4), argues that the evidence for matriarchal societies in prehistory is supported substantially by prehistoric myths and art. Myth also provides, he believes, evidence of the struggle leading eventually to the overthrow of matriarchy. His own researches and field work confirms the claim by Malinowski that the remnants of matriarchal societies remain in the twentieth century, for example in the matrilineal communities of Eastern New Guinea. Frankl argues that patriarchal societies are severely restrictive and inhibiting of childhood sexuality in a way that matriarchal societies are not. Melanesia has no taboos on sex in general. Children are freely initiated by each other into the practises of sex in their games. In this sexually open society violation of children is unknown. For Trobriand Islanders, where impermanent unions led eventually to the choice of a life partner, marriage was a means of assuring stable families rather than of regulating individual sexual life. Where the repressions and taboos of patriarchal society are not enforced infantile sexuality is openly manifested and people grow up without the sexual inhibitions and difficulties with intimacy we witness universally in patriarchal communities.

THE GREAT MOTHER

Certainly, a most significant reversal in the fortunes of the Male and Female Principles did take place at the dawn of history, around the turn of the second millenium B.C., heralding the rise of the Patriarchialism with whose history we are now only too painfully familiar. The Great Mother Gods, who had dominated the hierarchies of the gods until this time, fell into subsidiary roles (5).

Amongst the first signs of human existence on this planet are the small earth Venuses, figurines of pregnant women; women with the power to give life, women about to become mothers. The earliest form of deity, it seems, was the Mother God, expressing our desire for fertility on the land, in our animals and amongst ourselves. In ancient Egypt, for example, the Mother God, Isis, (identified by the Greeks as Demeter or Aphrodite) represented the rich plains of Egypt, made fruitful by the annual inundation of the Nile, which was Osiris, a Father God, separated from Isis by Set, the arid desert. The Egyptians had another fascinating Mother God, Maat (or Mat), whose name gave them their words for 'mother' and 'matter'. Egyptian traditions claimed she was begotten by breath, air - the principle of Life - and first appeared as an egg, whose shape gave them the figure 'O' - the Abyss of Nothingness or Emptiness, the pleroma of pregnant, undifferentiated existence. She was the God of truth and justice and her symbol was a feather, weighed on the scales of Judgment at the beginning of the journey of death.

The Virgin Mary, similarly, was believed by the early Church to have conceived at the impulse of a breath; and the Buddha, too, in the legends of his birth, was conceived by the breath of a white elephant (symbol of the Spirit). Some Arabic legends relate that Mary conceived by the breath of the angel Gabriel. In artistic representations of the Virgin Birth a dove descends upon her with the word or breath. The angel, like the dove, is a winged creature, whose natural element is the air. The dove was the bird of breath, air or soul, and was a symbol of the Holy Spirit - *to hagion pneuma* (the Healing Wind or Divine Breath). In the Gospels of Matthew and Luke it is the Holy Spirit who impregnates the Virgin Mary and in the numinous icons of Mother and Child, Mary and Jesus, the dove or the angel is a common motif, floating above the Virgin's throne.

When the first Christians came to Chartres they were astonished to find in a grotto, now part of the crypt of the Cathedral, a statue in wood blackened with age - older than Christianity - of a Virgin and Child. Tradition had it the statue was made by a Druid priest, to whom an angel had said a Virgin would give birth to a god. The statue was burned during the sixteenth century and the ashes scattered in the Loire. However, the sculptor of the tympanum of the door of The Nativity at the royal entrance to the Cathedral took the Black Virgin for his model; giving us, still, some sense of the power of the original statue. Mary sits, as she does in innumerable icons, on a throne, gazing forwards, with Jesus on her lap, between her legs - a vaginal phallus. Jesus is more a 'little man' than an infant.

Freud, on a visit to Rome, made a tour of its icons and was impressed with the fact that the child always appeared like a 'little man'. The icons represented, he thought, the universal human desire for a Good Breast. Whereas idols conceal what is hidden and perpetuate our conditioned vision, exalting and reinforcing that vision, icons point to what is hidden, what is invisible - that which lies trapped behind the face, the visage of the idol.

The icon of the seated Great Mother is the original form of the enthroned Goddess of antiquity. Eventually she becomes the throne. Her motherliness resides not only in the womb but also in the seated woman's broad expanse of thigh, her lap on which the newborn child sits enthroned (6). To be taken to the lap is, like being taken to the breast, a symbolic expression for the adoption of the child, and also of the man, by the Feminine. It is highly significant that the name Isis means 'the seat' or 'the throne'. (In German sitzen' 'to sit'; besitzen 'to possess'.) The king who 'takes possession' of the earth, the Mother Goddess, does so, literally, by sitting on her. Thus the king comes to power by 'mounting the throne', taking his place on the lap of the Great Goddess, the earth; becoming, as it were, her son.

When the Great Mother God receded into the background, the king sat upon the throne alone; the Great Mother had become the throne. Eventually, in the course of patriarchal dominance, the term 'to possess' a woman came to represent not only women as actual 'possessions' of men ('the owned of an owner'), but for the sexual act itself in which the man, now lying above (originally, perhaps from behind, to find the 'G spot'?), claims 'possession' in the most intimate relationship - but still revealing the primordial relationship in which the male obtains the earth from the female by being taken upon her lap. (In Indian coronation rituals the king was made to sit on a throne, which traditionally represented the womb.)

Ancient Mother Gods often contain the ambivalent qualities of She who causes war and destruction (her malevolence is caught vividly in the Hindu statues of the hag found in many temples) and of She who is the author of Love. The Mother God takes upon herself the archetypal qualities of omnipotence and omniscience. Like the mother who bears us, life and death are in her hands. She produces life, it seems, out of nothing and without her it cannot flourish. Parental handling of children prepares them for caring or for destroying. The offering or withdrawing of the vaginal or phallic breast provides a fearsome agent of control.

FROM THE UNREAL TO THE REAL

Although the Mother produces life, visible and tangible, conception comes via the male sperm. Eventually the role of men in the genesis of life was recognised. The 'breath' impregnating the female derives from the male. Breath, spirit, consciousness became Male; and matter, flesh, earth became Female. The gods gradually lost their individuality and in consequence lost also their power - transferred then to the act of sacrifice. Sacrifice compelled the gods, male and female alike, to accede to human will. Through the ritual of sacrifice we believed we had come to manipulate Nature. But sacrifice did not satisfy us for long and deeper yearnings beset the human soul. We desired union with the Ground of Being, Primary Narcissism, a return to the unselfconsciousness of our animal past; and longed for the unity beyond all multiplicity; for the One Reality beyond all existence. At first it was believed spirit, consciousness, emerged from matter; now we came to believe it was the other way around - that matter emerged from spirit (that essence preceded form).

The shift of emphasis is to be seen, for example, in the *Hymn to Primal Man* in the *Rig-Veda*, where matter is conceived as subject to change, whilst spirit is changeless. *Purusha*, the Male Principle, became a synonym for pure spirit and to complement him there was *Prakriti*, the Female Principle, who was matter. According to Zaehner (7), the whole trend of Indian religion changed with this new emphasis - the quest for immortality had begun. He feels that the famous prayer of the *Brhad-aranyaka* Upanishad is typical of this new trend:

> From the unreal lead me to the Real!
> From the darkness lead me to the Light!
> From death lead me to immortality!

Earth, the Great Mother, bore life; but it was with the Father, pure consciousness, that it originated. Salvation, spiritual freedom and enlightenment came to be understood as union with consciousness pure and simple, the unreflective consciousness of Primary Narcissism, discovered beyond our attachment to the Parental imagos in a 'return to the beyond of the womb', the Ground of Being. In this union (yoga) all the hierarchical complementary polarisations, Father and Mother, Male and Female, Good and Evil, Better and Worse, were reconciled.

Self-consciousness, with its ability to discriminate and measure, is a late evolutionary development. In the attempt to preserve our separation from Nature we have created cultures dominated by masculine values in which women and the Feminine Principle have been appallingly abused. Unbalanced by the complementary emphases of the Feminine Principle, these male values are ruthless and competitive, hierarchical and discriminatory.

Eating of the fruit of the Tree of the Knowledge of Good and Evil allowed us to begin a new and independent relationship with our universe; but it also brought death into the world - i.e. separation, alienation. Each human child would lose its innocence in the process of cultural conditioning, through the vehicle of the parents and the family, and be faced with the life task of regaining innocence. The parents would become vehicles of the culture and, unwittingly and inevitably, agents of separation.

Discriminating between Good and Evil, Better and Worse, Right and Wrong has permitted the development of our civilisation, science and technology. Our discrimination has allowed us to steal fire from the gods, but we have paid a dreadful price in our alienation from our own depths, from one another and our world. Men not only sat in the lap of the enthroned Mother God, from Whom they received power, but they removed her until all that remained was the throne itself. They not only 'sat upon' women and replaced them, they subjugated them in the world and took all visible, tangible power from them. The great icons remain, however, a challenging, covert reminder that power is not ultimately with men, but from the Mother. What was it that so terrified men and women alike that they colluded in this long history of repression? We are awakening, as we approach the new millenium, to the disastrous consequences of this repression and hopefully may now seek a new way of relating to one another as the Great Mother returns, perhaps, to share her throne.

THE SUBJUGATION OF WOMEN

Western history reveals the role of women from earliest times, in Greece and Rome, as subsidiary and inferior to that of men in society and even in the generally considered appropriate domain of the woman - within the home. Amongst the Greeks, for example, from Homer in the sixth century B.C. to Galen in the first century A.D. women were believed to be essentially passive and even the best of women would be inferior to men. Although Plato, in *The Republic* (8), writes of the equality of women, believing they should be educated like men and should be allowed to do as they wish, nonetheless considers they w o u l d perform the same tasks less well than men. Aristotle declared that women were inferior to men in every respect - anatomically, physiologically, and ethically.

In Roman society women entered their husband's household as a daughter, under their partner's authority. Although the death of a father left his daughters legally autonomous along with their brothers, unlike their brothers they were not invested with the power to hand on their estate (9). Many Roman women were able to engage in artisanal and commercial activities, but there were specific feminine trades: wet nurse, midwife, actress, masseuse, weaver, seamstress, washerwoman. In Homeric societies only legitimate offspring were entitled to inheritance. Illegitimate children from the concubines, providing 'recreational sexuality', commonly found (often several at a time in well-to-do households) in Homeric homes, were entirely without status. Already women were property, given with presents in marriage or bought in the slave market. Adultery here, as amongst the Semitic peoples since at least the time of Hammurabi, was an offence against property laws - not against the person, but against property.

Aline Rousselle (10) believes the letters of Musonius Rufus, a Stoic philosopher and teacher of Epictetus, exiled by Nero in 65 AD, represent a change in the fortunes of women and the quality of family life. Latin culture at this time had allowed upper-class women, expected now to be sexually inhibited, time for serious study and philosophical reflection. That women were capable of great courage was also recognised. Indeed, they were expected to face death without fear rather than bring shame on their household. Musonius expresses in his letters his belief that women have been granted the same faculty of reason and natural predilection for virtue as men. Although he still shares his culture's belief that women are weaker and must do, therefore, less arduous tasks, nonetheless he considers the possibility in some instances of role reversal. Musonius insists men should emulate the women's capacity for temperance, sexual self-control, and courage. They should not take advantage of sexual opportunity offered by slavery, but, again, practise self-control.

The recognition, reflected in the letters of Musonius, by his culture of women's ability to think, the admonition that men should renunciate sexual relations with concubines and the rejection of abortion and infanticide conspired to give new importance to the married couple and the large family.   Men who had large legitimate families demonstrated their capacity for fidelity and their desire for their wives.   It was now believed men could be faithful husbands to intelligent wives.

In the Christian era, since Constantine had forbidden men to keep concubines, husbands now entered into briefer sexual relationships with other women or had more frequent relations with their wives.   So exalted became the official, so-called 'orthodox' Christian view of marriage that adultery and abortion were considered   more serious crimes than murder.   Harsher punishments were inflicted for marital infractions than for the rape of a servant!

Oriental influences led to the practice in the Greco-Roman world of allowing women to become priests.   At first the early Church followed this model, especially amongst the Gnostics, who appointed not only women priests, but also women bishops and referred to God as Mother.   A new model of religious participation began to emerge, based on suffering for Christ and bearing witness to his 'Kingdom'.   The significant presence of women in the Gospels, especially at the crucifixion and Resurrection, and their roles in the spread of Christianity, described in Acts, brought a new egalitarianism for awhile.   Paul's influence here, especially if we take out the passages in his works attributed to Pseudo-Paul (the interpolators), reveals his treatment of them as equals and there is no sign that women's abilities were in any way considered inferior to those of men (11). Proclus of Constantinople declared: "Through Mary all women are blessed. No longer is the female accursed, because her race now has what it needs to surpass even the angels in glory."(12)

Amongst the Gnostics male-female opposition was abolished, women were made virile and a primordial androgyny was restored (13). However, by the second century the Gnostics had been persecuted almost out of existence and their writings proscribed;   and the 'orthodox' Church continued to subject and subordinate women within an established, male-dominated hierarchy.

MAKING SEX

In his fascinating account of the relations between sexual anatomy and cultural attitudes to sex and gender, Thomas Laqueur (14), relates the story told by an eighteenth century physician of a young aristocrat,   forced by family circumstances into religious orders, who came to a country inn where the innkeepers grieved the death of their only daughter. They asked the young monk to watch over her body through the night.   He was overwhelmed by the girl's beauty and took "the same liberties with the dead that the sacraments of marriage would have permitted in life".   Ashamed,   he left first thing in the morning, without waiting for the internment.

It was discovered, however, that the girl was not dead, but in a coma.   The delight of the parents was subdued by the eventual discovery she was pregnant. As soon as the baby was born, the girl was placed in a convent.   When the young aristocrat, now out of religious orders and into his inheritance, returned to the inn and heard of her predicament, he asked for and received her hand in marriage.

The physician, in relating the tale, asked his readers to conclude that only scientific tests can make certain someone is really dead. But his contemporary, Antoine Louis, a noted surgeon, came to a very different conclusion, arguing that no-one, physician or lay person, could have believed she was dead, having made her pregnant, since no woman could conceive without betraying her orgasm in the movement of her body. Without orgasm, declared a widely circulated text of the time, women would "neither desire nuptial embraces, nor have pleasure in them, nor conceive by them."

Within the short space of fifty years, however, medical opinion had so changed that Dr. Michael Ryan, writing at the end of the eighteenth century, included the story amongst a number of cases cited to demonstrate that orgasm was quite irrelevant to conception! A woman need feel no pleasure in order to conceive and need not even be conscious.   This recognition of the contingency of pleasure permitted the possibility of endless debate on women's sexual nature and from that debate emerged a commonplace cultural assumption: whilst men wanted sex, women wanted relationships.   Here was a complete inversion of the pre-Enlightenment belief, extending back to antiquity, that equated friendship with men and sensuousness with women.   Women, whose desires, it had been believed, knew no bounds, and whose reason offered little resistance to the power of passion, now became creatures untroubled by sexual feelings; and the presence or absence of orgasm became a biological sign of sexual difference.

In addition, the late eighteenth century saw another radical cultural change in the interpretation of the relationship of male and female bodies.   For thousands of years anatomists and theologians alike had expressed the universally accepted belief that women had the same genitals as men except that women had their genitals inside the body. There was actually only one sex, the male sex, of which women were an inferior variation.   Galen, for example, writing in the second century A.D., declared that women were essentially men in whom a lack of vital heat had resulted in the retention, inside the body, of the genitalia visible in the case of men. The vagina was an interior penis, the labia a foreskin, the uterus a scrotum and the ovaries were testicles.

Somewhere in the late eighteenth century our view of human sexual nature changed and writers now insisted on fundamental differences between men and women. In place of a peculiar determination to insist on only one sex, gradations of one basic male type, there arose a voluminous literature articulating sharp corporeal distinctions. A new model of radical dimorphism, of biological divergence and physiological incommensurability replaced the old one. However, it remained true, nonetheless, whether the one-sex or two-sex concepts were dominant, that sex was explicable only within the context of battles over gender and power. By the nineteenth century the cry went out from the members of the medical profession, confirmed by giants such as Charcot, Virchow and Bischoff, that claims for equality between the sexes were based on profound ignorance of the irrevocable physical and mental differences between the sexes and that these differences - the weakness and emotionality in particular of women - made inevitably for differences in social status and employment. This vision of the relationship of the sexes persists, despite the Feminist revolution, down to our own time. It is salutary to remember that the first woman to pass through the Royal College of Surgeons did so as late as 1947.

THE WAR OF THE SEXES

It has become common to note the mobility, emancipation, privilege of men in contrast to the confinement and reduction of women and to see men as sexually abusing, violent, abandoning, dominating and absent. We recognise how much of our political life is dominated by men and masculine (macho) values. The amount of physical violence perpetrated by men far surpasses that by women, which is miniscule by comparison. That men behave in such destructive and competitive and insensitive ways cannot but make us ponder what we are doing, generation by generation, to our male children.

It is becoming clear that the oppression and subordination of women is bad not only for women, but also for men. The dominance of men has impoverished their relationships with women with the inevitable consequence, according to Kristeva, that marriage has become "antinomic to love." The war of the sexes has estranged us in our most intimate areas of relationship. Cultural training forces little boys into stereoptypical prisons (the boy must not weep, or back down, reveal weakness or, until recently, contemplate certain professional possibilities, such as nursing - and so on and on) that are just as damaging to them as they will be to the women with whom they relate, and to their community.

A time has come, along with the development of the feminist movement, to recover some sense of the positive value of 'maleness', especially of the role of Father; and reach out to a side of the male parent which does not radiate castrating tyranny and abusing authority. We need to look at women and men, mothers and fathers, in ways that will help us nurture the best qualities and potentialities of each; to break free from the need to 'take sides'. As Andrew Samuels writes in *The Political Psyche* (15), we have become "caught up in a struggle between two gigantic, competing parents". The political logic of this, he says, is that it has become difficult for us to write about the positive, loving, flexible father and we are "cut off from the veiled symbolization of political regeneration that the father also carries."

The effect of the psychodynamic emphasis on the significance (especially since Klein, Winnicott and Guntrip) of the earliest relationships between the infant and the mother as primary caretaker, has, despite some efforts to make for more balance, left us with an inadequate account of the pre-Oedipal relationship of the child to the father - in particular the part played in human development by the direct relationship of the father's body with a baby. Clearly, also, at the present time depth psychology lacks an adequate approach to homosexual development and to the issues of homosexual parenting.

Depth psychologists (notably Winnicott, Lacan and Jung amongst others) have not paid sufficient attention to the cultural construction of gender and parenting roles. If we consider that the roles of father and mother are not biologically fixed either in our genes or in the unconscious (in the archetypes), we are moving to a point where everything we think about families becomes an open question. As Samuels argues (16), families with marginal, deviant styles may thus take on the role "of pathfinders, explorers of differing ways of running families and of thinking about them, a form of laboratory for the majority."

Single parents, for example, help us to see the "lack of nature" in the mother/father relation, so that we may ask the kinds of questions usually deflected by reference to tradition, biology, unconscious phantasy, archetypes and the like. Irigaray declared that western culture rests upon the murder of the mother (17): "The man-god-father killed the mother in order to take power ... And if we make the foundations of the social order shift, then everything will shift.

That is why they are so careful to keep us on a leash ..." Western culture also rests, of course, upon the murder of the father. (Alongside the Oedipal myth one should set the absence of Joseph, the father of Jesus, from the Crucifixion scene in the Christian myth. In the Gospels, as already noted, he is obliterated without mention.) Just as mothers and fathers may damage their children through passing on received stereotypes, so both fathers and mothers may play a valuable role in helping their children to become free of cultural conditioning; to be their own plural persons, who may grow and make life choices that are not predictable.

Emphasis on the pathology of the overtly abusing father draws attention away from the covert abuse of what Samuels calls a 'dry' father, who concentrates on getting 'the son of whatever sex' to conform to ideals and values held collectively by the community. He conforms to what a father is expected to do - deal with matters of conscience and morality. But the dry, passionless, way of attempting this, lacking a certain 'aggressive spirituality', raises massive problems for his children concerning the fate of their own aggressive impulses and phantasies. We are concerned here with the subtler abuse of our children, the abuse of conditioning them with received social stereotypes, values and ideals; making them, in Irigaray's terms, "captive to the law of the Same". We need to teach our children how to take risks, how - like the prophet, the poet and the lover - to be the ones who dare to be themselves. Protecting ourselves and our children, however unwittingly, from the threat of the Abyss by conformity to whatever gods of adaptation, means we share the ultimate fate of those who can only repeat and restate paths already opened up; that "erase the trace of gods who have fled."

After centuries of seeing women as 'the problem' - a trend easily recognisable in medicine, religion and art - men are now seen as 'the problem', depicted as sexually abusing, violent, planet-despoiling creatures. There is no doubt the image is a valid one. At the same time a different kind of man is emerging, the 'new man', who supports the rights of women and children, is ecologically aware and non-violent. A Men's Movement has arisen as a complement to the Women's Movement. Men can learn so much from feminism and work politically towards a better social and economic situation in our world, based on the attempt to achieve creative, non-violent, just, co-operative, non-hierarchical ways of relating and believing and new ways of organising family life.

One aspect of the Men's Movement which is disturbing is that revealed by Robert Bly (18) which, whilst rightly lamenting the desacralisation of our society, offers a mythopeic view of the family with little sense of the nuclear family as a source of oppression, as the vehicle of social conditioning and control. All right wing political movements express their concern with 'family values', meaning the confirmation of inhibiting, conventional, restrictive forms of traditional family life. Whereas, in fact, we have more to learn and to benefit from by considering all manner of alternatives; including, for example, those offered by the Masai, where married partners habitually have extra-marital relationships (sometimes actually living in the same home), where any children from these relationships are reared within the established family as if they were completely 'legitimate'.

Samuels (19) believes, further, that it is the transgressive styles of family organization, the so-called marginal or deviant lifestyles, that need to be affirmed and put at the centre of our thinking about the role of families in the future. What we learn, he declares, about child-parent relating, for example, by listening to two lesbians bringing up a son together, "is far more important than cliches about restoring the father's authority within the family, or achieving the recovery of distinctions betwen spheres of interest and influence within the family."

As Philip Larkin writes, laconically, in his poem *(20) This Be The Verse:*

They fuck you up, your mum and dad.
They may not mean to, but they do.
They fill you with the faults they had
And add some extra, just for you.

But they were fucked up in their turn
By fools in old-style hats and coats,
Who half the time were soppy-stern
And half at one another's throats.

THE CHILD AND THE WORLD

It is a dreadful irony that loving parents crucify their children in the name of love, believing they are doing the 'right' and 'best' thing for them. As Sartre has it in *Being and Nothingness* (21), we unwittingly educate our children into being ashamed of who they are. It is horrific and almost unbelievable how, generation by generation, families suppress their children into the collective vision, as if this is what parenting was about - teaching us to conform. The collective vision, upheld by fear of the Abyss beyond 'not belonging', terrified of difference or deviance, perpetuates the blasphemies of conformity. The collective vision becomes an idol outside ourselves to worship in the world, an idol hiding the truth, holding us above the Abyss. Whereas the good-enough family would become an icon, revealing what is invisible; leading us within ourselves towards the truth that is in us, and preparing us for creative encounter with the Abyss and a conseqent radical shift in our sense of identity.

Sometimes changes in the world about us, affecting deeply the culture in which we live, may throw us into unexpected deviancy. Katsuki Sekida, in *Zen Training* (22), tells of an eight year old Nisei girl, living with her parents and brothers in California at the outbreak of World War II. Government officials took them all away to a concentration camp. Until that time she had thought of herself as an American, just like her friends at school. She could not understand this sudden discrimination against her family, the painful sense of abandonment. Sekida uses the story as a dramatic illustration of one way out of so many possible scenarios in which children are betrayed. The family of the Nisei girl were eventually released and she was married. However, throughout her adolescence and young adulthood she was oppressed by the trauma of her experience as a child.

The Nisei girl went to live in Japan and read about Zen and tried to practice *zazen* by following instructions from her books. One day, quite suddenly as she was about to take a bath, she recognised that something had changed within her. The world, that had seemed so full of menace, now appeared friendly. Her oppressive depression lifted and she felt liberated from her burdens, happy and blessed. She decided to consult a Zen master about her experience and the roshi confirmed she had experienced *kensho*. Perhaps, without the dreadful experience of the concentration camp, she might never have come to *kensho*, since the imprisonment we all share through our universal alienation wthin the mores, might well have remained hidden behind the hard shell of social adaptation.

Our understanding of the relationship between adult pathology and childhood training has been greatly enriched by the explorations of psychotherapists and their clients. It might be said that psychodynamics has been obsessed with the early relationships of the child to parents, especially mother, and siblings. One of the most startling contrasts between contemplative procedures the world over, in different ages and climes, and the procedures of the depth psychologists is that whereas the psychodynamic therapists are absorbed with the individual experience of the client, the contemplatives saw the predicament of their charge against a universal, cultural backcloth, common to us all. And it is interesting to see how, as psychodynamic theory has developed, we have moved further and further into the early history of the child in our attempt to understand human develpment and pathology, towards the mysterious nothingness of the womb, towards the Abyss, towards common origins and predicaments.

During Freud's lifetime most psychotherapists believed psychodynamic methods were suitable only to neurotics and hysterics - and not to psychotic people and that exploration of individual trauma could fruitfully end at the Oedipal position. Therapists were embarrassed when regression did not stop at the Oedipal phase, but went beyond it, sometimes actually bringing psychotic episodes into the life of a client. Brilliant theorists, such as Melanie Klein and Guntrip, posited deeper, earlier positions - the depressive position and the schizoid position. Klein argued the most significant period in human development was the weaning period, from about four months of age. Some therapists (23) were brave enough to work with psychotic patients both individually and in group work, recognising the clear parallels between the descriptions of the struggles of the mystics, their behaviour and appearance at times on the Path, and their own observation of people struggling in psychotic episodes.

In therapy practised at depth over long periods the parallels become even more evident (24) and we find ourselves dealing with material for which there are no explicit memories and the client appears to be drawn inexorably to that shady nothingness we are calling the Abyss. The long process of education, of creating a viable Ego system as a defence against the threat of the Abyss, in order to fulfil the requirements of the Ego Ideal, to fulfil Oedipal expectations, leads to the paradox that I may have a sense of belonging only by sharing in my own alienation. It seems that whatever has happened to me as an individual is only a variation on what happens to all my peers. Ironically, as with the Nisei girl, the most evident, obvious and dramatic trauma may actually give me the kind of difference or deviancy which is my opportunity for release; since it prevents me from making satisfactory adaptation to the conventional and the normal.

Recently psychotherapists of various persuasion have come to recognise the political implications of these trends and discoveries; a rediscovery of the contemplative understanding of the universal social and cultural implications of their personal struggles. Geraldine Finn, for example, in *The Politics of Spirituality* (25), declares that politics speaks directly to the "space-between being and being as: this fertile, disruptive, unpredictable space of the relation with an otherness which ex-ceeds established categories of prediction and control." Conservative politics (and some so-called radical politics), she says, "speak to this space in order to contain, deny or negate"; whereas genuinely radical and progressive politics speaks to affirm it. Authentic radical politics must begin there, in the space of "deviation and differance; the space from which the 'arbitrariness' of political divisions and classifications and the incommensurability of being and thought (of my being and my being a woman, a lesbian, a black, a Jew ...) are both visible and lived, visible because lived."

However, writes Finn, it is unfortunate that radical politics seldom recognises "the place of its origin" because it is bereft of a language with which to do this. In consequence radical politics tends often, disappointingly, towards the same kind of "political positivies and 'final solutions'" as the conservative regimes they wish to transform. They do this unwittingly through "obscuring once again that experience of excess - of the space between reality and representation, being and being-as - from which they can be deconstructed and resisted."

THE HOLY FAMILY: IDOLS AND ICONS

"Whereas," writes Marion (26), "the idol results from the gaze that aims at it, the icon summons sight in letting the visible be saturated little by little with the invisible." The idol, he says, gathers only "a foreign brilliance", whereas the icon unbalances human sight in order to "engulf it in infinite depth", marking such "an advance of God that even in times of worst distress indifference cannot ruin it." Saint Paul applied to Christ (Col. 1: 15) the formula: "icon of the invisible God." This formula, argues Marion (following John of Damascus), should be applied to every icon.

The Holy Family of the birth story myth in the New Testament is an icon which has been idolised. It is idolised when treated as a historical drama, rather than as an existential model. It is idolised, this Holy Family, when it is embedded in culture and politics as an idealised norm (overlooking the conflict Jesus had with his own family and his declaration in Luke 14: 26: "If any one comes to me and does not hate his own father and mother and wife and children and brothers and sisters, yes, and even his own life, he cannot be my disciple."), obscuring the clues which might lead us to the invisible, towards the Abyss. We worship and encourage the worship of the idol in order to conform and belong, passing it on generation by generation, crucifying our children.

The icon of the Holy Family, however, persists and lives on as an icon, revealing the invisible where it may, and speaking out the existential truth about our predicament, even where the organised religions of the world do their best to hide it again and to interpret it within the mores and the crippling hierarchies of sameness, pressing us deeper into our alienation.

The Christmas story, an essential ingredient in the myth of that first century Holy Family, presents a polarisation - on the one hand is the Baby Jesus, representing the Christ Child (symbol of our potentiality, our Core), supported by shepherds, angels, wise men, and, above all, by loving parents; on the other hand is Herod and his minions (symbols of the powers-that-be; of the Ego/Super Ego alliance; of the tyranny of the surface 'self' within the soul), who then, as now, are willing to murder children in their beds. Herod initiates the Massacre of Innocents; yet Herod, too, was once a baby: the Christ Child (the Logos), is present also in him, as it is in everyone - and the Christ Child is present (incarnate) also, in the soldiers, who are willing to commit murder.

Why does Jesus grow into the stature of a beautiful adult, so that the glorious potentiality of the Christ Child is recognisable, whereas Herod grows into a murderer, tyrant and sadist? Out of the same human potential something very different has arisen.

We say, well, Jesus was Good and Herod was Evil. But what does evil mean? It means, as the myth informs us, to be divided against the Christ Child, i.e. split off from my Core. Evil is the dangerous sourness of life split against itself. Jesus becomes Whole (holy) and beautiful; Herod becomes split, divided, evil and ugly. Why?

To answer that question we have to see evil as something I am, not something I do. Evil deeds are the signs, the outward wickedness, obvious evidence of inward disorder. I say obvious because evil is not always obvious. Jesus, indeed, said we were all evil and that no-one, including himself, was good - except God. We are all somewhat split or separated from our potentiality, the glory we have it in us to become: "Your righteousnesses are as filthy rags!" How that must have hurt people who liked to count themselves good, even something special - "not like this tax-collector!"? People enjoy living on high moral ground, from which they may condemn others, play the blaming game, because they are under inward pressure to dissociate themselves from their own error (sinfulness). It is this splitting under the education of social conditioning that produces evil. Jesus has managed to become free from this conditioning; whereas, Herod, alas, like most of us, has not. Becoming free from that conditioning and discovering the power, the Spirit, that flows from the inner Christ Child, is the universal religious quest to which we are all called by the Christmas message.

Recently two boys in puberty were convicted of the abduction and murder in Liverpool of a small child. A friend of mine lives in the area where these children lived. Her son, in his late twenties, also brought up in that area, said: "They should be tortured and strung up. I wouldn't have done that when I was eleven years old." We can see him, in these words, distancing himself from what has taken place; and expressing his horror at the possible identification of the murdered boy with his own small child? I am good and they are evil, he is saying, along with many other people, of course.

"Bring back the stocks and the birch," said one Member of Parliament - I am good, they are evil. "They knew right from wrong." Of course they did. "The church is not teaching right from wrong," he accused in the very next breath. But the children knew right from wrong. Not that the church gets much chance to teach anything - and what it does teach is not popular. People do not want to hear we are all sinners - there but for the grace of God go any of us. People want to hear plenty of blame thrown about; plenty of aggressive expression of sadism, as they climb to the dangerous, self-righteous heights of moral high ground held by the Moral Right. Whose side are they really on - that of the Christ Child or that of Herod? Forgive, says Jesus, forgive seventy times seven. Love your enemies - throw a stone only if you are without sin yourself. That would be even more dangerous now than it was then - since clearly a lot of people are absolutely sure they are without sin! "Father forgive them for they know not what they do?" But they knew right from wrong, didn't they? They knew it was wrong to crucify people, didn't they?

They believed, of course, that their horrific, sadistic cruelty was justified because the Christ Child grown up was evil - because the Christ Child grown up was teaching things they didn't want to hear - like helping your enemies, the Samaritans; being compassionate towards the occupying army; saying God loved everyone and that we should do likewise. Herod (symbol of the Ego-Super Ego liaison) desires to murder the Christ Child because that Christ Child (Id figure) will be his undoing. Herod is controlling master of his world (the surface, conscious world of the Ego system) and the birth of the Christ Child threatens his dominion. So it is in all of us. We have to give up our vaunted autonomy to the movement of the Spirit if we are to become free - and the Spirit blows where it will. Who knows where it comes from or where it may go?

My friend says 3-4 year olds, where she lives in Liverpool, throw stones at people's ankles and then run away. She and some colleagues maintain a half-way house for children in the area - children who regularly spend nights sleeping in telephone booths, kicked out by parents. She hears people say: "They should kick the parents out as well, so they can have a taste of it." These children, of course, will grow up to be the kind of parents who kick out their children in turn. "Aren't we all responsible for what we do?" Who can deny it? "Do we not all know right from wrong, unless insane or badly brain damaged?" Yes, we do. "Then we should 'crucify' or 'massacre' people who offend against us - against what we see as right and wrong? They should suffer." The logic is inexorable.

One in seven children in the city run away from home. One in seven teenagers in the area commit suicide. The Samaritans tell us that every three and a half hours 150 people in Britain think of suicide and two actually do it. They receive one call every 12 seconds. Over Christmas, as we celebrate the birth of the Christ Child and receive pictures of the Holy Family through the post - that is, more specifically, between Christmas Eve and Holy Innocents Day (the festival commemorating the massacre) - they will receive eight thousand calls a day.

A big clue to whether we become whole or whether we become evil, or of the extent to which we become evil, is given in the myth - the ability of parents to care and be aware of their children and to express their love for them: the resources they have for doing that. And, clearly, it has not to do ultimately with wealth or poverty; but with the resources within themselves - which deprivation, of course, may undermine and demolish.

We are a very unhappy society. We just don't like to face it; we especially don't like to face what we do with our children; we especially don't like to face at Christmas - Happy Family Time - what we do with our children. So we concentrate on the plum pudding, the tinsel and the presents, listen to the Queen (the physical embodiment of the Mother of the Holy Family) and don't strain our imagination wondering what might be the spiritual significance of the Christmas myth. It is so much easier to place the story in the past, and literalise it as a historical event in the life of Jesus, rather than as part of a myth as relevant to our modern situation as it was two thousand years ago.

What is the explanation of evil? Our Member for Parliament, intent on distancing himself from the problems, played the blaming game again - it is caused by Video nasties, by lack of discipline at home. We should introduce, he said, harsher legislation to deter - the birch, harsher prisons, stocks, hanging. Now, who is speaking here? "Kill the little bastards! Give them some pain!" Who is speaking here? Is it the Christ Child or is it Herod?

We're all in the same boat, is what Jesus says. We should have compassion for those trapped in an evil net and recognise where the sadism comes from and how much we all share of it. Instead of distancing ourselves from the ills of the world, the Christ Child tells us how much we are all a part of it, and yet also part of the good of the world; the world's hope lies in our essential nature, corrupted though it may become; hope lies in the promise of its restoration into the glory we have it in us to become - Christ-like. Out of the greatest darkness light may shine; in the midst of death we are in life; out of winter will rise the spring; from the tomb emerges the life of resurrection (transformed consciousness).

Herod cannot destroy that child, though he may inhibit it. The Christ Child is forced into Exile in Egypt, the traditional 'land of Bondage'. But every year, the hope of its return, its home-coming, is reaffirmed at Christmas, when the recurring presence of the myth asks us to choose whose side we are on - that of Herod or that of the Christ?

JERUSALEM

The icon of the Great Mother, sitting on the vast throne of the Eternal Feminine, attended by angels and cherubim, golden light circling her head, with her young son on her lap, makes visible what is invisible, offers possibilities beyond our envisaging. The political implications for a world that has torn her from her throne and put a precocious patriarchy precariously in her place, with its Ego-centric, macho values struggling for pride of place amongst the idols of the world, are mind-blowingly enormous. The icon turns everything on its head - the hope of the world lies not with its Kings and Conquerors, its Priests and Prelates, its Unity and Conformity, with Pomp and Power; but with the deviant, the misfit, the poor, the oppressed, the dispossessed and the humble; the victims of patriarchy - all those with whom this astonishing Christ Child identified and whom the worldly despise.

William Blake's great hymn, 'Jerusalem', is the prelude to a vast poem, *Milton*, and has clear parallels with another vast poem, *Jerusalem*, both written and engraved between 1804 and 1820. These poems took as their theme the Fall of Humanity. Blake observes the throes of the early Industrial Revolution and declaims against the poverty and injustice he sees, against the cruelty and inequality. The first part of the hymn asks if there ever was a time when the Holy Lamb of God was seen here? Was there ever a golden age? And the second part is an invitation to commit ourselves to the vision of the possibility of creating an age of justice and equality, of mercy and truth, of peace and love.

Albion, the Child of God, in Blake's work is male and a symbol for humanity crushed by patriarchy. Albion (the Roman name for Britain), who represents human potential and suffers or triumphs in each one of us, is in bondage everywhere, says Blake, corrupted, abused, labouring in slavery at the Mills, like

Samson; dancing the Dance of Eternal Death - i.e. spiritual darkness. Jerusalem, the symbol in Blake of regeneration, is female. She is radiant Femininity, the agent of reconciliation and restoration. Rejoined with Albion in a spiritual marriage, she brings the sense of unification, of belonging to one family on earth and in heaven, out of which true reverence for all life, and for difference, emerges. Jerusalem represents the power, energy and compassion of the Eternal Feminine and it is only as she merges in an androgynous union with Albion, the Eternal Masculine, that together they may dance the Dance of Life.

NOTES FOR CHAPTER FOUR

1. Laura Esquirol. *Like Water For Chocolate.* Black Swan Books. 1994. Pp. 14 - 15 and 113.(c) Seventh Dimension Entertainment Co.Inc. 1993. Published by Transworld Publishers Ltd.

2. Lionel Casson. *Ancient Egypt.* Time-Life International. 1966. P. 80.

3. Michelle Perrot and Georges Duby. *A History Of Women.* Harvard University Press. 1992. P.XX.

4. George Frankl. *Archaeology of the Mind.* Open Gate Press. 1990. Vol. 1. Pp. 1-7.

5. See Erich Neumann. *The Great Mother.* Princeton University Press. 1974 ed. Pp. 55 - 68; 91 - 92; 330 - 335.

6. Neumann. Ibid. P. 98

7. R.C. Zaehner. *Concordant Discord.* Oxford. 1970. P. 74

8. Plato. *The Republic.* tr. Cornford, F.M., Oxford. 1942. Pp. 142 ff.

9. Perrot and Duby. Ibid. Pp. 97; 135;

10. Aline Rousselle. *Body Politics in Ancient Rome.* Fm. Perror and Duby. Ibid. Pp. 296 ff.

11. See David C. Doel. *That Glorious Liberty.* Lindsey Press. 1994.

12. Sermon 5, "Praise of the Holy Virgin and Mother of God Mary, Patrologiae Grecae65, 720B, fifth century.

13. Pagels, E. *The Gnostic Gospels.* Weidenfeld and Nicholson. 1980. Pp. 99-101.

14. Thomas Laqueur. *Making Sex.* Harvard. 1992. Pp. 2-4.

15. Andrew Samuels. *The Political Psyche.* Routledge. 1993. P.126

16. Andrew Samuels. Ibid. P. 147

17. Luce Irigaray. 'He Risks Who Risks Life Itself', tr. David Macey, fm. *The Irigaray Reader.* ed. Margaret Whitford. Blackwell. 1991. Pp. 47 and 213.

18. Robert Bly. *Iron John.* Element Books. 1990.

19. Andrew Samuels. Ibid. P. 189. See also *Beyond Monogamy.* J.R. & L.G. Smith. John Hopkins. 1974.

20. Philip Larkin. *Collected Poems.* Faber and Faber. 1988. P. 180.

21. Jean Paul Sartre. *Being and Nothingness.* Methuen. 1966 ed. P. 222

22. Katsuki Sekida. *Zen Training.* Weatherhill. 1975. Pp.137 ff.

23. cf. Francis A. Macnab. *Estrangement And Relationship.* Tavistock. 1965.

24. see David C. Doel. *The Perennial Psychology.* Lindsey Press. 1990.

25. Geraldine Finn. The Politics of Spirituality fm *Shadow of Spirit.* Berry and Wernick. Ibid. P. 114

26. Jean-Luc Marion. *God Without Being.* Chicago. 1991.Pp. 17 and 24. page 86

CHAPTER FIVE

ALIENATION, PORNEIA AND THE MORAL RIGHT

I have a vision of the future of a world where all the necessary sex education will be available to everyone, thus there will be no more sexually transmitted diseases ... Fetish lingerie and sex toys will be freely distributed to all people. People will be able to make love without touching if they choose. Men will be able to have multiple orgasms without ejaculating, so that they can maintain erections for as long as they want. Women will ejaculate. It will be possible to make love anywhere in public, and it will not be impolite to watch ...

Post Porn Modern
Annie Sprinkle (1)

He who knows the male, yet cleaves to what is female
Becomes like a ravine, receiving all things under heaven.
And being such a ravine
He knows all the time a power that he never calls upon in vain.
This is returning to the state of infancy.
He who knows the white, yet cleaves to the black
Becomes the standard by which all things are tested ...
He returns to the Limitless ...
The more prohibitions there are, the more ritual avoidances,
The poorer the people will be.
The more 'sharp weapons' there are,
The more benighted will the whole land grow.
The more cunning craftsmen there are,
The more pernicious contrivances will be invented.
The more laws are promulgated,
The more thieves and bandits there will be.

Lao Tzu - Tao Te Ching (2)

Christ frequented the disturbed and the delinquent not because he felt sorry and wished to do good to them, but because he knew that they would be the most receptive to the Word. Through their less well-organised defences the Word could penetrate and lodge. Childen too, if young enough.

Rosemary Goring

From The Living Rock-Face (3)

One day Jesus was preaching in his home at Capernaum (Mark 2, v 1 ff.) and the house was packed with people, so there was not room even in the doorway. Four men came, carrying a paralysed man on a bed or pallet, using it like a stretcher. When they saw the crowd and could not gain entrance by the door they climbed onto the roof of the house, cut a space in it and lowered the man to the floor. Jesus does not say: "What have you done to my roof?" or "Why couldn't you wait until I'd finished?" He is impressed by their enterprise.

"My son," he says to the paralytic, "your sins are forgiven."

Now what had that to do with anything? Had the paralytic not come in hope of being healed of paralysis? Jesus, it seems, sees clearly and instantly into the man's predicament. He is paralysed by guilt. Jesus extends forgiveness, as he believes God will forgive no matter what the man has done, out of love (Agape). Accepting the authority of Jesus the man is healed of his guilt and its psychosomatic effects.

"Take up your bed and walk!" Or "Carry now that which has carried you." The man is affirmed and energised. He picks up his pallet and leaves.

The scribes accuse Jesus of blasphemy - forgiving sins, when only God may forgive sins. Which is easier, asks Jesus, to forgive sins or heal a paralytic - surely it amounts to the same thing? Jesus invites Levi, the Tax Collector, along with other 'sinners' for a meal in his home. "Why does he eat with such people?" ask the Scribes. Jesus replies: "Those who are well have no need of a physician, but those who are sick; I came not to call the right(eous), but sinners."

Jesus goes on to break the Law in various ways - including healing on the Sabbath and condoning the plucking of ears of corn on the Sabbath. The objecting Scribes belong to the Moral Right(eous), whose Righteousnesses, says Jesus, "are as filthy rags". Those on the moral right wish to distance themselves from the 'sinners', but Jesus identifies with them and reveals his love for them. The moral right take a traditional conservative stance in order to be 'in the right' and so free from the acknowledgment of guilt. They are not, in fact, free from guilt, but have blocked off their sense of guilt by managing to appear 'in the right'. They are as paralysed by guilt as the paralytic, except they are paralysed in their minds and in their relationships with people. Being 'in(on) the right' not only provides a defence against guilt, but also a barrier against the confusion of not knowing clearly what is right and what is wrong. If there were no law to guide us, we would not know when we were in the right or in the wrong and so could, unwittingly, come under condemnation.

Paradoxically, however, although the Scribes are completely sure they know what is right and what is wrong, they did not know what was right and wrong. With hindsight we can see they were in the wrong and that Jesus was right because his behaviour flowed not out of guilt, out of a desire to be right, but out of love (*Agape*). The moral right manipulate people through their guilt, use it as a political weapon and create a politics which is divisive rather than healing, confirming the paralysis rather than healing it; a politics which pereptuates division rather than promote reparation. Since, as Jesus says, no-one is free from sin, the pretence of being without sin leads inevitably to hypocricy.

As Anna Marie Smith points out in *New Right Discourse on Race and Sexuality* (4): "The intolerant always misrecognise themselves as 'tolerant'; they do so not only to legitimize their exclusions within a liberal-democratic framework, but also to transform their own violent exclusions into a reasonable discourse which would otherwise be unbearable to themselves." The flight to the heights of the moral right is a flight from a guilt too painful to bear. Yet it is only through that guilt we may find our way into freedom and realise our own potentiality. Guilt paralyses our freedom to be ourselves and yet, at the same time, is an invitation into our own depths. As Heidegger has it (5): "Being guilty is more primordial than any knowledge about it ... the 'summons to Being-guilty' signifies a calling forth to that potentiality-for-Being which in each case I as Dasein am already."

EVIL AS ALIENATION

In classical Christian theology Evil is a universal human condition of separation or alienation from the Ground of our Being; the condition of a psyche which is split, divided against itself. The contemplative traditions of the great religions of the world assume we all become divided against ourselves - that we lose the simple unity of innocence and that our life task is to regain innocence. The word devil has a Greek root meaning 'the Accuser' (like a prosecuting counsel in a court of law); and a sanskrit root from which we get also the word dual - meaning to divide. The Devil is the Divider, the internal Accuser whom Freud named the Super Ego - popularly referred to as that Voice of Conscience, "which doth make cowards of us all".

Evil is the condition of alienation, separation, spiritual exile, psychic splitting, produced in us from infancy by the conditioning influences of the world. In two classical texts Jesus says: "If you, being evil, know how to give good gifts to your children ..."; and "Call not me good, no-one is good except God."   We are all, even Jesus it seems, suffering the division of Evil, alienation or exile from our own potentiality, and our spiritual or psychological life task is to reach that goal of unity or integration, that wholeness or holiness, which is represented by the elusive concept of the Good; i.e. in Christian theology by the Christ and in Buddhism by the Diamond Body of the Buddha.

The term 'Sin' is used by contemplative theologians to refer to our 'existential Death' and the estrangement or alienation it produces. Paul Tillich (6) described Sin as separation. To be in the condition of Sin is to be in a state of separation. This state had three aspects: there is separation within an individual life, separation of each of us from our own true selves and the separation of all human beings from the Ground of Being. This threefold separation, Tillich wrote, constitutes the state of everything that exists; it is a universal fact: "Existence is separation! Before sin is an act, it is a state."

The Buddhist term *Boho*, usually translated into English as 'sin' similarly meant 'alienation from the Buddha' and is conceived as a condition common to us all. From this alienated condition enlightenment will liberate us.

Contemplative theologians, Depth Psychologists, Existentialist and Postmodern Philosophers and Marxists all discuss the concept of alienation. They do not always mean precisely the same thing when they use the word, but they have it in common that they believe human beings become estranged from each other and from the natural world by social influences. They see alienation as an impoverished condition, a kind of Exile, from which human beings need to be set free.   The term 'alienation' may be traced through the writings of Grotius, Hobbes, Locke, Rousseau, Fichte, Schelling, Hegel, Marx and Heidegger.

Amongst these European philosophers it has two chief functions, both deriving from Middle English usage (7). One function has to do with property: to the transfer of the ownership of something from one person to another. It is used in this sense frequently by Marxist writers. The second traditional usage referred either to loss of consciousness or to estrangement in personal relationships. *Alienatio* mentis or simply *alienatio*,   could be descriptive of a loss of consciousness caused, perhaps, by a blow or an epileptic seizure and the verb, *alienare*, became associated with the cooling of personal relationships and hence with personal separation.

In Middle English literature it was used primarily to refer to the separation of human beings from God.

The French derivative, *alienation*, means both estrangement and insanity. In German the word *Entfremdung*, usually translated into English as 'alienation', also has its roots in the late Middle Ages, where, once again, it was used to denote our separation from God. When Luther made his famous translation into German of the Greek New Testament he used *fremd* to translate the Greek *appellotriomenoi* in the fourth chapter and eighteenth verse of Paul's letter to the Ephesians:

They are darkened in their understanding, alienated from the life of God ... (RSV)

It is ignorance (cf. ignore-ance as *avidya*), due to the hardness of our hearts that, in Paul's view, sustains our alienation. Alienation for the contemplative teachers who succeeded Paul involves separation from God and from loving relationships with people, since in an alienated condition we are in Exile in the world and the love of God (*Agape*) cannot flow through the soul. This is the condition or state of Sin - a kind of spiritual death in which love atrophies. Luther was expressing a universal religious teaching when he asserted it was necessary to die to the death of Sin - a "dying to death" - in order to live richly.

EXILE

Michael Ignatieff, discussing his physical exile in our country, suggested that Exile is a symbol for all our lives, since growing into adulthood is itself a kind of Exile from childhood and youth. People who move to foreign lands are thrust into a recognition of their existential Exile by the need to adapt to a new environment. They are thus prompted into an awareness of the sense of Exile we all carry around within us, although we may remain unconscious of it. This sense of Exile, argues Ignatieff, comes from not letting go of your old self; a 'letting go' allows one's roots to be transformed. People tend either to cling to the culture they have left behind, as people sometimes cling to their own background and manner of up-bringing, or they try to abandon their roots in a desperate attempt to belong in their new world; just as sometimes people rebel against their origins in order to secure themselves in a new social milieu, when they move across the class structures of their society. If we hold to our roots but allow them to be transformed by their transplantation in a new culture, we never lose them, but find instead they become an ever richer part of our living.

It is holding on to ourselves that produces eventually our sense of Loss, since Life demands movement and change. If we are unable to move with our time and place we find ourselves in Exile even in situations where we have lived our whole lives.

The word Nostalgia, frequently used of the Exile's yearning for her home, has two roots - *Nostos*, meaning home and *Algo* meaning to return. Nostalgia is a yearning for the lost innocence and unity of childhood, projected now into the past - the delights of Eden - captured beautifully in A.A. Milne's delightful phantasy, *The House at Pooh Corner* (8). Christopher Robin is leaving the forest and no-one knows why. He and Pooh would no longer go 'just nowhere' and do 'just nothing', listening to all the things you can't hear 'and not bothering' - which always led to the enchanted place!

"I'm not going to do nothing any more," says Christopher Robin.

"Never again?" asks Pooh.

"Well, not so much. They don't let you," answers Robin.

Christopher Robin, of course, is 'growing up' and will lose touch with childhood. A man I worked with would weep whenever he read this story to his children.

"Pooh!", says Robin, "You will understand, won't you?"

"Understand what?"

"Oh nothing."

He laughed and jumped to his feet. "Come on".

"Where?" asked Pooh.

"Anywhere", said Christopher Robin. So off they went together:

But wherever they go, and whatever happens to them on the way, in that enchanted place on the top of the Forest a little boy and his Bear will always be playing.
Our nostalgia, sense of Exile or alienation, is a recognition of the loss of that Child's world and represents the need to find a way back into the world of the Lost Child - to learn how to do nothing and go nowhere in total absorption (learning how to play is the goal of therapy, according to Winnicott). As the Buddhists say:

Sitting quietly, doing nothing, the spring comes and the grass grows by itself.

To be in Exile is to be a restless wanderer, an agitated spirit, always busily 'doing', going 'somewhere', seeking to be in control and always, therefore, at odds with the flow of the ever moving river of life. Falling in love is one of the routes we travel to find a way Home, find the place where love is; learning how to love is a finding of one's way Home, since to be able to love we have to be open to the moving moment, become vulnerable, unsure of where things are going or where we are. Indeed, no-one is more in exile or more isolated in the world than people who know exactly where they are and who manage to fulfil the Oedipal expectations crystallising in their Ego Ideal. There is no despair, as Kierkegaard argued in *Sickness Unto Death*,(9) like the despair of the one who, having desired to become Caesar, now has indeed become Caesar - for the more we are Caesar the less we are ourselves.

Fulfilling our phantasies may prove the saddest of all experiences, since when that fulfilment does not bring the protracted joy and peace we desired, but leads only into the emptiness we had hoped to avoid, deep disillusionment is bound to overtake us. If our phantasies have been realised and brought in the end only grief, where is there to flee now from our inner desert?

In classical Christian theology Evil was given no reality of its own, no actual existence except as the absence of Good; in the way that darkness exists only as the absence of light. Goodness was holiness or wholeness; whereas Evil was life divided against itself - disunity. Sin was the word used by contemplative theologians to describe this divided condition of separation or alienation and it was out of the condition or state of Sin that particular sins arose. Theologians were not claiming that wickedness or evil deeds had no reality of their own, of course, but that the condition of being in Sin, resting in the darkness of evil, continued only in the absence of the illuminating and transforming light of the Holy Spirit, as agent of transformation within the psyche. Separated from the inner world of the Kingdom of God, where the Spirit moved, we lived in Exile in the world and inevitably found ourselves at odds with life, sinning unwittingly, no matter how hard we might try to be good. In the unity of the Spirit, however - possessed by the vision of that inner kingdom - it was believed we could not err. Just as evil deeds arose out of the divided condition of the psyche so, out of the unity or wholeness of the person, would spring the good fruits of wholesome inter-personal relationships.

Jung believed the description of evil as *privatio boni* something of a euphemism, hiding the harsh, horrific reality of evil; especially as it had erupted in our own time in the two World Wars and the holocaust. The Shadow side of human nature balanced and complemented consciousness, he believed, in the way Satan balanced and completed the Christ in a quaternity that included evil, giving it a place in spiritual reality. Unrecognised, remaining unconscious, the dark, sadistic, unacceptable side of our nature would eventually explode in destructive chaos; but recognised, made conscious through integration, however, it gave zest, verve and creative power to individuals and their communities. Any individual wishing to have an answer to the problem of evil, he wrote in his autobiography, has need, first and foremost, of self-knowledge. One must know relentlessly, he declared, how much good one may do, and what crimes one is capable of. Both were elements within our nature and both are bound to come to light if we wish to live without self-deception or self-delusion. In the contemplative literature, Jung's emphasis was anticipated in the insistence that growth in sanctity leads to an increasing recognition of one's sinfulness. It is the developing sense of one ís human frailty and disorder, the growing consciousness of the Shadow, which characterises the first stage of the contemplative path, known as the Way of Purgation.

When the American gangster, Charlie Berger, stood on the scaffold, he looked up at the sky and said: "It is a beautiful world, isn't it?" Then the trap fell away from his feet. The words represented an acknowledgment of the total waste he had made of his life by pursuing the criminal career he hoped would make him wealthy, potent and influential. How human the remark is! When we pursue energetically our Ego/Super-Ego directed life goals, in search of this or that bauble, we are estranged by our own directiveness and by the concomitant anxieties maintaining our crippled sense of identity. Only when we stand aside from these restless pursuits, are we able to become engaged with the world around us and share the vision of the world as beautiful in and for itself.

FREUD AND EVIL

Freud was asked to explore the question of whether people who behaved in 'evil' ways were possessed by evil, taken over by some force extraneous to themselves. Freud was commissioned to study the life of the murderer, Ivan Poderjay, who had lived with his wife for many years in a Viennese flat, equipped as a torture chamber. Poderjay was a masochist, who submitted himself to torture from his wife, whom he called Count John. He acted out various sexual phantasies with her collaboration. However, he fell into serious financial difficulties and tried to resolve them by marrying bigamously a rich American woman, whom he murdered on their transatlantic honeymoon, cutting the flesh from her body and feeding it through the porthole to the fishes of the deep. Was he evil before the murder or did he become evil at the time he committed the murder? Freud felt Poderjay had remained the same rather silly little confidence trickster he had always been - the grandiose label of 'evil' kept falling off. The nature of evil is not to be discovered in this or that offence against law and humanity, however bizarre or horrific, but in something hidden more deeply in our minds, splitting the psyche against itself; something profoundly divisive against the very roots of our being, for which even the most horrific crimes are but signs or pointers.

Nietzsche believed the history of criminal families led back always to an individual too strong for his or her particular environment. The criminal, he argued, was often a dominant person, craving a sense of achievement or purpose; someone whose life represented thwarted growth. Crime brought meaning and excitement, even a sense of worth and purpose, into a frustrated and alienated life. Hitler was an ambitious, dominant person, terrified in his teens that he would be a nobody. Hitler had an appalling, fear-ridden childhood - continually subjugated and humiliated (see Alice Miller and Robert Greenblatt (10)). He brought into adulthood an enormous well of unassimilated suffering and rage. One reason we crave purpose is to exercise freedom, and what we describe as evil behaviour often appears as an acting out of a desire for freedom that has run amok - an intense, egocentric desire for freedom not recognising the boundaries of other people's needs, other people's freedom. His complete insensitivity to the freedoms and sufferings of other people and the enormous number of people murdered because of his obscene policies makes Hitler the arch villain of our century. Like the serial killers of our time, he was was trapped in a schizoidal universe, where people were no longer real; serial killers often refrain from killing when potential victims become too real, too vivid to be treated as objects.

But we all have this capacity to treat people as objects. So-called normal people wish to distance themselves from Hitler or the serial killers by denouncing them as 'evil'; but we should recall how 'normal' people found the bombing of Hamburg quite acceptable, despite the murder of elderly folk, men, women and children living in its houses; affirmed the dropping of atomic bombs over Nagasaki and Hiroshima; and still support political policies designed to maintain and promote the unjust, appalling, indefensible gulf both in Britain and abroad between the rich and the poor.

ALIENATION IN POLITICS

Simply by being human, it seems, existing in the world, standing out, we become alienated by the very acts of rational discrimination which make us human and distinct from the natural world. As we cling to the received images of ourselves and our world that hold groups of people together against the threat of regression, a political leadership emerges to promote a misguided sense of self-interest perpetuating our alienation and making it difficult to recognise and tolerate difference. A deep paranoia against difference asserts itself in political decision and has, for example, sabotaged the work of the United Nations to realise the dream of the aftermath of the second World War to create a fair and just world, where peace would reign.

The creation of a global market has brought about the paradox that whereas the United Nations was concerned to help the Third World, we now have negative equity, by which the rich countries actually take more wealth out of the Third World than they put into it. We have exacerbated the problems of the global poor both in the Third World and even in the wealthy nations themselves. Different kinds of tyranny, whether that of small oligarchies or the tyanny of majorities in democratic countries, privilege the wealthy and diminish the poor, creating cruel discrimination, enormous social injustice, wastage of talent, and threat to life and health - whether in debt-ladened Latin America, the declining rust-belt communities in Europe or the starving in the Horn of Africa.

A common political weapon in the repression of unpalatable truths that might spell trouble for the status quo is the use of censorship - the withholding of information. In Britain, for example, censorship was used in the twenties and thirties to hide the extent of civil disturbance, rioting as protest against the misery of widespread unemployment. Steve Humphries and Pamela Gordon, in *Forbidden Britain* (11), exploring the phenomena of Rioting, Sexual Abuse, Delinquency, Unemployment, Homelessness and Adultery in Britain between 1900 and 1960, reveal how Government censorship made their task extremely difficult:

> Feature film or newsreeel coverage of all the issues we explore was either
> banned or closely controlled. The press did cover subjects like riots,
> juvenile crime and affairs in some detail, but the reporting was often
> extremely biased and distorted.

In race riots, for example, the overwhelming reaction of the press was to blame

Britain's black community for the violence they suffered and the most taboo subjects like incest, adultery and child sexual abuse were "considered so shocking they were rarely reported on or even spoken about."

The censorship of sexual issues was an especially sensitive political area. Both within religion and politics there appears to be a ratio between censorship and the right or left wing persuasions. It was during a Labour Government, for example, that Divorce proceedings were permitted legal aid, allowing poor people to choose divorce. During Thatcher's conservative government sexual censorship, especially on the television, increased. One would, of course, expect that regression was a more seriously disturbing possibility for people attempting to maintain or re-inforce the mores of an earlier age.

A friend of mine researched in belly dancing in the Middle East and discovered the regulations governing what could and could not be revealed during belly dancing varied according to the politics of the regime. The more restrictive and right wing a regime, the more regulations there were governing this exotic and erotic art. Similarly, the TV crew, documenting the making of a soft porn calendar in Cuba, who entitled their film *The Cuban Nipple Crisis,* discovered there were regulations, carefully policed, about what proportion of the outer ring of a woman's nipple might be published in a photograph. In Mao's China young couples caught in pre-marital sex were separated, publicly humiliated and sent to labour camps. In Bangladesh victims of rape are whipped and those accused of adultery are stoned to death.

We live in the astonishing situation where, on television, we are 'permitted' to watch people shot, stabbed, beaten up, mangled in horrific car chases, tortured and drowned, but we are not allowed to watch people 'make love'.

A fascinating volume produced by postmodernist feminists and edited by Pamela Church Gibson and Roma Gibson, entitled *Dirty Looks* (12), opposes the censorship of pornography. They dislike and condemn pornography which demeans women or makes use of children or animals, but are in favour of more pornography by women for women or by gay people for gay people; pornography in particular as an art form.

Three distinct positions are customarily recognised on pornography - liberal, moral right and feminist. The liberal position defines pornography as sexually explicit material designed for sexual arousal, arguing there is no scientific evidence for pornography causing harm in society. Whilst it offends many women and men, it brings harmless pleasure to others. The moral right movement define pornography as representations of sex removed from what is believed to be its legitimate function and context in procreation within marriage. Pornography is considered, by them, to be a threat to traditional family values. Not only have the moral right brought pressure to bear to censor any public display of naked bodies or of premarital or extramarital sex, but also to suppress information on birth control, abortion and sex education in schools; condemning, in particular, homosexual imagery as threatening family life and of creating general social and moral decay. An authentic concern for family life is deflected by the pornographic issue from the real issues of poverty, affordable health care, homelessness, money for public education and social services, and the care of sufferers from AIDS.

The feminist critique of pornography condemns the sexism and exploitation of women represented in mainstream pornographic material, which is also frequently racist. However, the recognition that obscenity laws enforced by a male dominated judiciary always served to suppress the work of those fighting for women's own control of their fertility and sexuality, many feminists began to take a new attitude towards pornography. Believing that men's cultural contempt for and sexualisation of women long predated the growth of commercial pornography, they have seen it as a product of the relative powerlessness of women and that emphasis on the role of pornography detracts from the more serious issues of mysogyny within our most respectable institutions, including politics, law, medicine, the church and the family. What women need, according to feminists opposed to anti-pornography crusades, is not more censorship but more sexually explicit material produced by and for women, more open and honest discussion of all sexual issues, alongside the struggle against the subordination of women.

Significantly, research has revealed a positive correlation between equal opportunities for women and higher rates of pornography. Countries like Sweden and Denmark, with permissive attitudes to pornography compared with, say Britain and North America, also have higher levels of equal opportunity for women and lower levels of violence against women (13).

Feminist sexual politics has been greatly influenced by women such as Annie Sprinkle, who tells us with a smile that when her feminist mother would joke with her whether she would grow up to be a whore or an artist, "She was exactly right!" (14). Annie Sprinkle's work has demonstrated the political context in which we consider questions of art and obscenity. She claims there is no longer any secure category into which we may confine sexual obscenity. As gender and sexual identities have become more politicised and 'speaking sex' important to gay, lesbian, bisexual, transexual and sadomasochist activists alike, drawing clear lines between what is dirty and what is clean, what is properly brought on scene and what should be kept off (ob)scene no longer seems relevant to Annie Sprinkle and many other feminists of like mind.

Their sympathies increasingly are with Phyllis and Eberhard Kronhausen, psychologists who organised the First International Exhibition of Erotic Art in Sweden in 1968, declaring in their catalogue that erotic art expresses the demand for sexual freedom - a freedom vital to individual happiness and mental well-being (15):

In that sense, erotic art carries a truly revolutionary message: it demands no less than extension of freedom, not only in the sexual area, but in every sphere of social life.

PROSTITUTION

The word 'pornography' derives from the Greek words *porne*, meaning 'female prostitute' and *graphos,* meaning ' writing'. *Pornographos*, however, referred in antiquity simply to a subcategory of biography - tales of the lives of the courtesans - which did not necessarily contain sexually explicit or sexually arousing material at all. The word *porneia* was used of those who consorted with *pornai* (Women prostitutes) and *pornoi* (Men prostitutes) and then of 'fornication' and then of 'habitual immorality' and then of 'sin' - thus completing the common confounding of sin and sexuality.

Annie Sprinkle's versatility as prostitute or 'sex-worker', erotic dancer, educationalist, entertainer and creative artist, reminds one of the Greek hetaira, Aspasia, a contemporary of Plato, who ran a gymnasium for prostitutes, where she taught rhetoric, philosophy, religion, poetry, not only to prostitues, but also to statesmen, including Pericles and Alcibiades; and to philosophers, including Socrates. Annie Sprinkle is like a re-incarnation of Aphrodite, the god of Love, whose flesh was as important as her spirit and who simultaneously taught the receiving and the giving of pleasure and the receiving and the giving of knowledge.

In *Prostitution: Soliciting for Change* (16), Nikki van der Gaag suggests that, like any other oppressed minority group, prostitutes have conflicting voices and experiences - whether heterosexual, bisexual, lesbian or gay. Some see prostitution as a personal tragedy, some have chosen the profession freely and find their work personally as well as financially rewarding. All of them, she says, oppose and resent the stigma and the constricting laws made against them. Most of the time their voices are drowned by those of the moral right. Kate Miller, a prostitute, who has spoken effectively for the decriminalisation of prostitution argues prostitutes supply a valuable service and deserve the same respect as anyone else in society. She pointed out in a TV interview how she had worked for ten years in the defence industry and declared: "if that isn't classed as immoral earnings, I don't know what is." Prostitutes often argue they are also therapists. Indeed, sexual therapy, inside the fringe of respectability, now includes paid 'sex surrogacy'.

In many parts of the world prostitutes are at last speaking out and beginning to be heard - in Brazil, Britain, Thailand and North America. An international 'Whores Congress' was held in 1985 in Amsterdam, at which male and female prostitutes reclaimed the word 'whore' as lesbians have reclaimed the word 'dyke'. They also set up a World Charter for Prostitutes' Rights, in the hope it will eventually be accepted by the United Nations.

Ironically, the 'sense of sin' gripping the imagination of so many so-called 'religious' people, potentially such a powerful force for reparation and healing in our world - in fighting poverty and discrimination, tyrannical hierarchical structures and the scourge of war - attached itself to sexual appetite. As Tannahill argues in *Sex and History* (17): "By some mysterious alchemy, sexual purity came to neutralise other sins, so that even the moral oppression and physical barbarity that became characteristic of the Christian church in later mediaeval and Renaissance times scarcely appeared as sins at all in comparison with the sins of sex and heresy."

REPARATION

To combat Evil in the world Goodness must surely have more power and force than is given it by those who merely live 'morally right' within the mores. Goodness is not a dreary tendency to behave ourselves, to live within the conventions, to avoid breaking the law; but rather it is the ability to behave freely in a way that gives a vision of freedom to others and respects their freedoms in turn. Great artists, musicians and poets are those who lift our minds and hearts by their work to a vision of what it means to be free. They are able to live through time and yet give us a vivid awareness of the things that are timeless - a vision of the Eternal Now.

Before we may find our way Home - to the place where love is - we have to recognise our isolation, our existential Exile, our condition as Evil. Before we may know what it is to be at one within ourselves, we have to acknowledge our fragmentation. It is not only a matter, either, of recognition - we have to embrace our alienation, our isolation, and live with it in an accepting spirit.

Yalom quotes in the section on 'Isolation' of his *Existential Psychotherapy* (18) a passage from Robert Hobson:

> To be a human being means to be lonely. To go on becoming a person means exploring new modes of resting in our loneliness.

Yalom likes the phrase 'exploring new modes of resting in our loneliness' and suggests it contains the germ of the clinical problem in psychotherapy:

> rather than 'rest' the psychotherapy patient writhes in loneliness. The problem seems to be that the rich get rich and the poor get poorer. Those who can confront and explore their isolation can learn to relate in a mature loving fashion to others; yet only those who can already relate to others and have attained some modicum of mature growth are able to tolerate isolation.

Yalom recommends patients spend increasing amounts of time in isolation, learning how to allow their own depths to speak to them, permitting unconscious material to rise into consciousness. Toleration of increasing amounts of isolation will also permit them to discover their own inner resources of courage and strength. No solution to isolation may be found in the overt world, in seeking friends or building families or empires at work, being 'in the right', since that isolation is a part of our existenz as separate universes in time; but we may, paradoxically, by confronting our inner loneliness and suffering - resisting the temptation to flee - discover our unity with all things.

In the knowledge that our aloneness and suffering is a part of our common humanity, shared with everyone, comes a growing sense of unity with others and enhanced compassion for them. In addition will emerge an awareness of inner unity and strength, a sense of integrity and of being loved by Love. Our developing knowledge of our own inner isolation is part of the spiritual journey into that true wilderness, which the western contemplatives called the Dark Nights. Beyond the Dark Nights, in the Abyss, they taught, lay the experience of union with the Ground of our Being.

Anthony Storr has written about the role of isolation in the lives of highly creative people in *The School of Genius* (19), where he argues that solitude has an extremely stimulating effect on creative activity, its erudition and style. In solitude, he contends, men and women are able to change their attitudes, come to terms with loss, encounter their deepest feelings and make use of their creative imagination. He is adamant it is through embracing isolation, so dreaded by people, that highly creative activity is fostered.

Psychotherapeutic experience confirms the discoveries of the contemplatives: the more we flee from our inner isolation, our alienation, our condition as Evil, the more out of touch with reality we become, the more alienated from the world in which we live. The two classical phobias, agoraphobia and claustrophobia, represent projections of the Ego's terror at its own existential condition. In claustrophobia the person is projecting an unconscious awareness of being enclosed, encapsulated, isolated; and in agoraphobia the person is projecting the terror of moving out of that inhibiting, but reassuringly familiar interior prison.

Our experience of cultural training in childhood prepares us to live in and through our phantasy worlds, imprisoning us in our phantasies, rather than teaching us to use our phantasy life as a creative tool for relating more intimately and meaningfully to ourselves and our world. We are taught to use our phantasy life to distance us from our world, rather than to explore more intimate ways of relating with the world. Trapped in phantasies designed to protect the Ego/Super Ego liaison - this present sense of identity - we dissipate our energy in maintaining or pursuing the phantasies until life becomes drab and without stimulus, since all the stimulus is coming from within the narrow boundaries of the liaison and all our energies drained in maintaining it - 'the narrow climes of our prison'. Life is then devalued by us - our own lives and the lives of other people. Criminals react to this devaluation through their crimes - crime gives purpose, excitement, a sense of power and meaning and offers quick solutions to life problems. Respectable people react to it by ambitious pursuit of status, wealth, affirmation within the mores.

MELANIE KLEIN AND ORIGINAL SIN

Many theologians in the twentieth century tried to make theology meaningful to contemporaries by re-interpreting myth and doctrine in a manner appealing to modern minds with sophisticated knowledge of evolutionary theory, depth psychology, genetics, physics and cosmology. The myth of the fall of the walls of Jericho, for example, was explained by the physical laws of sympathetic vibration; the parting of the Red Sea was due to a tidal bore; the Virgin Birth was either not quite necessary to faith or was to be understood as an answer to Gnosticism (although there were those suggesting it might not be entirely biologically impossible, since some frogs were known occasionally to be self-productive!). The turning of water into wine at the Cana wedding was explicable because the cool water, tasting gently from the wine-impregnated bottles, would be the perfect drink for people with jaded palates; the Resurrection appearances became collective visions or hallucinations; and the Emptiness of the Tomb was the work of the Essenes, who snatched the body.

Original Sin, too, was rationalised in various ways: as a reference, for example, to factors in the environment of the growing infant effecting it deeply, but of which it was unaware - syphyllis, for instance, at work in the womb due to a sexual liaison before the child was conceived; inherited disorders such as muscular dystrophy; a country at war; the poverty of the society or the particular family; mental illness in one or both parents; the follies and misconceptions of the mores of the community where the child is born; and so on.

The writings of Melanie Klein were a gift to some of these theologians, since she declared the infant came into the world already possessing sadistic impulses and 'bad objects' from its experiences in the womb. The doctrine of Original Sin was now understandable under the rubric of depth psychology and sheltered by the authority of its discipline.

Melanie Klein was a gifted clinician who, through her work with children and her acute observation of infants, contributed important new dimensions to psychodynamic theory. She taught that the Child's experience remained a part of its present mode of relating to people and things throughout development into adulthood. Klein gave clinical support to the view of Existentialist philosophers, that human beings are the creatures whose past is always in the present. Human dis-ease began in the womb and was modified as time went by through the interaction of the child with parents, siblings and the world beyond the home. These experiences and their effects on the psyche did not disappear as we grew older, but remained dynamically alive in the individual in adult life.

If the child had more 'good' experiences than 'bad' it would grow up more or less adapted to the community, but if the 'bad' experiences outweighed the 'good' ones the person would, either as a child, or later as an adult, be unable to adapt and would reveal serious mental and/or asocial disorder.

When the child's caretaker (prototypically the mother in most societies) satisfies the baby, argued Klein, they are 'at one' and the baby does not feel the mother as separate. However, when she cannot satisfy the baby's needs, she or her breast are experienced as distinct; as the first separate psychological objects. The baby responds to this sense of separation or distinction with anxiety and also, for the sake of comfort, recreates the mother for itself in phantasy. In this way, Klein taught, the baby forms a separate area within itself, becoming the basis of the person's Ego or sense of self. The original unity of the psyche is now divided and increased fragmentation or 'splitting' takes place as the Ego learns how to disown parts of itself felt as dangerous or unacceptable. The Ego thus protects itself by projecting split off parts onto the world of people and things or by introjecting to its sense of identity values and judgments received from significant people in its life. Every infant, Klein claimed, will inevitably introject, project, and split its objects, since these psychic manoevres are essential to the establishment of a separate, rational and imaginative Ego. But an excessive use of these defences will produce serious disorder.

Through the work of depth psychologists such as Melanie Klein, theologians gained a fresh perspective on the doctrine of Original Sin and learned to interpret the allegory of the Fall in a manner more meaningful to their contemporaries without debasing or abandoning the ancient myths, poetic language and imagery of religion.

THE DEVELOPMENTAL STAGES OF INFANCY AND CHILDHOOD

The universality of our Fallen condition, emphasised by great religious poets and theologians in all cultures down the ages, is acknowledged in our own time by the depth psychologists. They see a human world where all of us are inevitably repressed or inhibited, split and fragmented, by the conditioning influences of the culture as it comes to us primarily through our Parents; but also, of course, through the media and education. Ironically, the very defences we use to establish our separate sense of identity, including the acquisition of language, although they rob us of our primary unity or innocence, are nonetheless necessary, these psychologists believe, to our development as individual, self-reflective, imaginative human beings.

Phantasy, for example, is not merely an escape from reality, though it may be used entirely in this way, but is, rather, a constant and unavoidable accompaniment of real experiences, always interacting with them and providing us, in consequence, with the invaluable gift of imagination. Melanie Klein suggested the very origins of thought itself lie in the infant's attempts to test phantasy against reality and that the richness, depth and accuracy of an adult person's thinking will depend on the quality and malleability of her unconscious phantasy life and her capacity to subject it to reality testing.

The most critical period in our development is generally considered by depth psychologists to be the weaning months; the earliest stage of personal development described by Klein as the paranoid-schizoid position. The anxieties of the Child during this 'position' and its reactions to them are crucial, she believed, to the quality of its psychic maturation. Most infants, of course, do not spend the whole of their time in anxiety states, but in favourable circumstances sleep, feed, experience real or hallucinatory pleasures, gradually assimilating their experience and integrating the Ego. But all infants do have some periods of anxiety and the anxieties and defences at the nucleus of the paranoid-schizoid position, although crucial, are in themselves, she claimed, a normal, usual, inevitable part of human development.

THE CREATIVE VALUE OF DEFENCES

One of the achievements of the paranoid-schizoid position is splitting, allowing the Ego to emerge out of chaos and to order its experiences, to begin to make sense of its world, a necessary precondition of later integration. It is the basis of what will, hopefully, become the faculty of discrimination; the key to the passage from the world of the animal to the human world as we learn to distinguish 'good' from 'bad', 'right' from 'wrong', 'better' from 'worse'. Here, as the Hebrew poets in the story of Adam and Eve and the Buddha in his Four Holy Truths clearly recognised, lies the hub of the problem of the human spiritual condition. We lose our Innocence by making these discriminations, which split and fragment us, but they are inevitable and even necessary to our adjustment to community living, to our development as separate individuals. We then have to spend the rest of our lives trying to find our way back into Paradise in the hope we may rediscover lost Innocence - that is the heart of the religious quest.

Picasso, in his mature years, visited an exhibition of children's art in London and was astonished at the freedom and spontaneity of the young artists. He remarked it had taken him all his life to paint with that same freshness of vision - to recapture Innocence in his painting. The inevitable and necessary splitting of the psyche, whilst it makes us human, at the same time interferes with our ability to be at ease with our instinctual life and at home with natural spontaneity.

Melanie Klein believed the ability to pay attention, to suspend one's emotion and form intellectual judgments, could not be achieved without the splitting manoevres begun in the schizoid position - what she called "a capacity for temporary reversible splitting." Moreover, Klein declared, some degree of persecutory anxiety is a necessary precondition for being able to recognise and react to situations of danger. Without the defence of idealisation, she taught, we would not be able to fall in love or appreciate beauty or form political ideals. Projective and introjective identification are defences allowing us to empathise with other people's condition and are the ground out of which the child's ability to form symbols arises.

After the Schizoid Position comes the Depressive Position, roughly between eighteen months and three years of age, and then the Oedipal position, roughly between two and a half and five years of age. In the Depressive Position the young child has to negotiate the hurdles of envy and jealousy, discovering it is the same person - himself - who loves and hates the same person - his mother. S/he is then faced with conflicts appropriate to his or her own ambivalence. This change in the state of the Ego, wrote Klein, brings a change in the focus of the child's anxieties. In the Schizoid Position, the main anxiety, she argued, was that the Ego will be destroyed, but in the Depressive Position, the child's chief concern is that her own destructive impulses have destroyed or will destroy the one she loves and depends on for survival. Throughout this period there is ordinarily a strengthening of the Ego, allowing the child to establish a firm relationship with the real world. Klein believed that if the depressive position has been adequately worked through the difficulties encountered in later development will not be of a severe, psychotic nature, but of a milder, neurotic form.

Reparation and restoration were ever present opportunities, Klein believed, for the growing individual. They were achieved largely through the experience of mourning; of enduring the grief, guilt and pain blocked off, locked up in earlier, unassimilated experiences. As human beings, either in childhood or in adult life, go through repeated experiences of mourning and separation, loss and recovery, the Ego becomes enriched, and self-confidence increases as well as the belief in one's ability to love and a trust in one's potentialities.

Amongst the most significant blocks to integration are our manic defences against pain and grief. These manic defences are affirmed and deepened by the cultural expectations and mores of our communities, with their emphases on material success, achievement in education or commerce, social status and the significance of money. However, even these defences, too, have a creative aspect to them, since they provide us with the energy and verve we need to engage fruitfully with our world. Our defences are not destructive or evil in themselves, but only as they interfere with the expression of repressed parts of our nature; inasmuch as the defences are not balanced by their complements.

NAKED AND UNASHAMED

A man I worked with talked without pause throughout the first few sessions. Then, during one session, he stopped speaking for several minutes. Tears rolled down his cheeks as he confessed how deeply ashamed he felt in the silence, as if he were now naked and I would despise what I saw. Words covered him up like clothing. He hid behind language. Without the words he was something to be despised. Without the words he was so vulnerable anything might happen to him - and whatever happened was bound to be 'something dreadful'. His thought processes, as he expressed them in language, protected him from the Look, which had despised and reduced him in infancy and which now he transferred to myself.

Because we have internalised the Look - a sadistic, moralising, harshly judgmental Look, passed on in the name of education or caretaking or religion - we have a reduced sense of our own inherent worth; that we are the precious childen of the living God, the hairs of whose heads are numbered; loved with a love that passes all understanding. The Lost Child, coming to the river bank in the myth of Saint Christopher, out of the storm of its grief and anger, has lost all the rich power of childhood, the fresh vividness of lively imagination, the amazement at the wonder of the world, the keen curiosity to explore. The self is locked in a prison-house built with bricks of shame and bound by bars of mistrust, held by the strong ropes of perpetual cerebration and locked with a key that is, like the one in the myth of Iron John, hidden under the parental pillow.

The Lost Child comes to the River, out of the Storm, in deep trouble, to the place of decision. Whether to venture into the unfamiliar, unknown world of the River - into the water element to struggle with dangerous currents, the pull of the rapids, the risk of submersion and drowning - or whether to return to the world of the Lost Child, which at least is known and familiar and appears safe to the Child, if only the storm will pass? Whether to push on into the fearful ambiguity of the world of Unknowing, where something dreadful is bound to happen - or to return to the agitated use of roles to support and fill out the sense of emptiness and loss, that is the question; whether to be or not be. Whether to risk that shady world beckoning from the Abyss, of being rather than doing; or whether to return to the doing world and its innumerable defensive roles: a return to being businessperson, parent, spouse, academic, layabout, the one who knows, the one who never knows, the knight in shining armour, the damsel in distress, the clown, the victim, the tyrant, the one who is good and never tells lies, the delinquent, the professional, the one who has all the goodies and must be envied, the one who gives up everything for others? Whatever roles have given comfort to the imprisoned Ego, struggling to find a place of rest behind the bars, life brings it eventually to the uncomfortable dilemma of the flea on the hot griddle - when it is up it must come down and when it is down it must jump up.

NOTES TO CHAPTER FIVE

1. Annie Sprinkle. *Post Porn Modernist*. Torch Books. 1991. P.13

2. Lao Tzu. tr. Arthur Waley. *The Way And Its Power*. Longmans. 1956. Pp. 178 and 211.

3. Rosemary Goring. From *The Living Rock-Face*. New Times Press. 1995. P. 21.

4. Anna Marie Smith. *New Right Discourse On Race and Sexuality*. Cambridge. 1994. P. 19.

5. Martin Heidegger. *Being and Time*. SCM. 1962. Pp. 332/333.

6. Paul Tillich. *The Shaking of the Foundations*. Pelican. 1966. P. 156

7. See Richard Schacht. *Alienation*. Allen and Unwin. 1971. P.2 ff.

8. A.A.Milne. *The House At Pooh Corner*. Methuen. 1979.Pp. 168 ff.

9. Soren Kierkegaard. trl. Lowrie. *The Sickness Unto Death*. Doubleday. 1954. P. 152.

10. See Alice Miller. *For Your Own Good*. Faber. 1982. with its vivid description of Hitler's appalling childhood. And see *Love Lives of the Famous* by Robert B. Greenblatt. MTP Press. 1978. for comments on Hitler's childhood and its relationship to his sexual perversions as an adult. His niece, Geli Raubal, stressed it was of utmost importance to Hitler "that she squat over his face in such a way that he could see everything."

She committed suicide after two years of his attentions. In his relationship with Rene Mueller Hitler pleaded with her to kick him, which excited him sexually. She committed suicide after knowing him but a short time. Almost all the few women who were intimate with him attempted or succeeded in committing suicide (P.67). Hitler was a grim example of the damaged, deviant pervert, who brings out into the open the covert sadism of the whole community. He rose to power on the support of a virulent nationalism and anti-semitism, endemic in his society. His brilliance as orator and political strategist allowed him to express and exemplify for so many people the common fear, indignation and hatred fostered in a Germany seriously deprived under the terms of the Versailles Treaty. Hitler, it seemed for so many of them, offered a messianic solution to their dire social and economic ills.

Incidentally, Greenblatt comments in his epilogue (P.135) how a sociological report on the clientele of prostitutes in Washington, D.C., revealed sixty per cent of them were "politicians or political power-brokers".

11. Steve Humphries and Pamela Gordon. *Forbidden Britain*. BBC Books. 1994. P. 6.

12. Ed.Pamela Church Gibson and Roma Gibson. *Dirty Looks*. British Film Institute Publishing.   1993. Pp. 1 and 6-9.

13. Pamela Church and Roma Gibson. Ibid. P. 18

14. "   "   "   "   "   "   P. 176

15. "   "   "   "   "   "   P. 151

16. Nikki van der Gaag. *Prostitution*: *Soliciting for Change*. New Internationalist. February,   1994. Pp. 4 ff.

17. Reay Tannahill. *Sex in History*. Abacus Books.1981. P.150.

18. Irvin D. Yalom. *Existential Psychotherapy*. Basic Books. 1990. P. 398.

19. Anthony Storr. *The School of Genius*. Deutsch. 1991. page 93

CHAPTER SIX

RESURRECTION AS TRANSFORMATION

The root of the chestnut tree plunged into the ground just underneath my bench. I no longer remembered that it was a root. Words had disappeared, and with them the meaning of things, the methods of using them, the feeble landmarks which men have traced on their surface ... Never, until these last few days, had I suspected what it meant to 'exist'. I was like the others, like those who walk along the sea-shore in their spring clothes. I used to say like them: 'The sea is green; that white speck up there is a seagull ... Things have broken free from their names. They are there, grotesque, stubborn ... I am in the midst of things that cannot be given names. Alone, wordless, defenceless, they surround me, under me, behind me, above me. They demand nothing, they don't impose themselves, they are there.

Jean Paul Sartre
Nausea(1)

Suddenly my spirit did break through the gates of hell, even into the innermost moving of the Deity, and there I was embraced in love as a bridegroom embraces his dearly beloved bride. The greatness of the triumphing that was in my spirit I cannot express either in speaking or writing; neither can it be compared to any thing but that wherein life is generated in the midst of death. It is like the resurrection from the dead.

Jacob Boehme
Confessions (2)

During deep meditation it is possible to dispel time, to see simultaneously all the past, present and future, and then everything is good, everything is perfect, everything is Brahman ... I learned through my body and soul that it was necessary for me to sin, that I needed lust, that I had to strive for property and experience nausea and the depths of despair in order to learn not to resist them, in order to learn to love the world, and no longer compare it with some kind of desired imaginary world, some imaginary vision of perfection, but to leave it as it is, to love it and be glad to belong to it.

Hermann Hesse
Siddhartha (3)

Helen had driven hard for three or four hours on a very hot day. She was hassled and fretful - late for an important appointment. Suddenly, on the road in front, appeared a hobgoblin. Sensibly, she pulled into a lay-by. When she looked back down the road the hobgoblin had disappeared.

She told her partner, John. He said: "How did you know it was a hobgoblin?"

"It just was."

She remembered it looked like a picture she'd seen of a hobgoblin in an illustration of John Bunyan's famous hymn about hobgoblins and foul fiends.

"Hob," John said, with the cynical rationality of a grand disbeliever, "means 'of the hearth'. What would a hobgoblin be doing on a main road?"

"How should I know?" she replied curtly, as one who has seen and therefore knows. "But that's where he was."

On a bright summer's day in 1572 learned scholars met in Bologna to discuss an encounter that had caused a stir in the area. On the 13th May a peasant, driving his oxcart across a field, almost ran over a small dragon, about a yard long. The stir was caused by the fact that the dragon had only two legs, whereas everyone knew dragons had four. Was it a migrant? Perhaps a flying dragon from Tartary, except it had no wings? Or perhaps the product of an unnatural mating - like a griffin?

Most people in our time, suffering the inhibitions of a modernist and post positivistic vision, would be astonished by a group of learned people engaging in serious discussion concerning the nature of non-existent creatures, whose proper habitat was mythology rather than zoology. The mediaeval scholars, of course, did not make this distinction. Dragons, hobgoblins, unicorns and the like belonged to the world between existence and non-existence - like God and the Devil, the angels and seraphim. They did not belong to the reality of the world of tables and chairs and gate-posts, but they did belong to the reality of the non-real world, to the reality of the supernatural world, which engaged with and intertwined with the reality of the natural world. Non-realism, like post-modernism, has a long, long history.

God, the Scholastics taught, could not be known in Her essential Nature, but only as an image appearing either in vision or dream - i.e. in the real-unreal world between things that exist - that is, stand out - in the world of space and time, and the timeless, spaceless world that Jacob Boehme, for example, called the

Ungrund, the Abyss, the indefinable matter of the universe, the Ground of our Being. Not unlike the way we now conceive of particles as existing in a world where the laws of the   general theory of relativity apply and, at the same time, existing in a world where the laws of the special theory of relativity apply - a multiverse?

A vision is a projected dream (opening itself, said Boehme, within us like a growing plant), and lends itself to the vagaries of dream interpretation. The hobgoblin, for example, exists as a symbol for a displaced aspect of one's self; a vivid image of a living fragment of the psyche. The world between existence and non-existence, as it breaks through the barriers of our sense of identity, the boundaries of consciousness, is still, as it always was, a lively aid to the integrative processes of our minds.

In 1734 the famous Swedish naturalist, Linnaeus, visited Hamburg, where the Burgomaster had a specimen of a seven-headed dragon in his collection - a Hydra. Linnaeus was invited to examine it. He congratulated the proud owners on their remarkable 'fake', a skilled concoction of skins from snakes and the heads and feet of weasels. So outraged were his hosts, Linnaeus felt it wise to quit Hamburg immediately!

There is clearly a difference between a 'genuine' hobgoblin and one that has been constructed from wire, glue and papier-mache.

"You had a hallucination," John said to Helen. "It was the heat and the fatigue - all the stress of driving."

Okay! But a hallucination, or a vision (*per imaginatio* as the mediaeval scholars would have said), is that not real in the non-real world of the imagination?

Perhaps John was right and the Hobgoblin did appear out of the stress of driving. Maybe her unconscious was sending a warning - it's time to rest, time to stop driving, before you have an accident. Maybe the hobgoblin is also a warning against more subtle forms of 'driving' -   like giving so much significance to a business appointment you push yourself beyond reasonable limits.

Maybe Helen was driving herself in all the sorts of unreal ways we do in modern society under the enormous, unreal pressures to get on, compete well, survive amongst all the unreality of those twin imposters, as Kipling called them, success and failure. Even the insistence that the goblin was a 'hob' goblin might not have been without its unconscious justification, since our driving, anxious, and manic behaviour, frequently does affect the 'hearth' - the very heart of our homes.

The slaying of the dragon is one of the most powerful images of mythology. Being slain is the primary role or destiny of dragons, as they appear all over the world. Amongst the hundreds of heroic dragon slayers are Herakles, Alexander the Great, King Arthur and Saint George. Slaying the dragon did not mean simply the heroic triumph of good over evil, it meant also a heralding of dramatic change, since behind the dragon - in the deep, dark cave or at the bottom of the well - lay enormous treasure.

Dragons take many forms in the world today. Some are obvious, like devouring tyrannies sucking the blood of their people; the exploitation of the poor and underprivileged; the obscene amassing of dreadful fire-raising, over-kill weapons. Some dragons, however, are more subtle and dwell hidden in the recesses of our minds; the product of social training, nurtured by the mores. They are not real, as sticks and stones are real; but in their non-real reality they are as active and effective in our world as the most tangible elements in our environment, such as the wind and the rain. In our dreams the confronting of our dragon still may represent the imminence of significant change in the dynamics of the dreamer's psyche and still give access to 'spiritual treasures'.

It's long overdue we should surrender our narrow vision of reality 'out there' and give attention seriously once again, to the realities within us; those belonging to that deep inner world we call the (Kingdom)Commonwealth of God, the rich, supernatural world of the human psyche. Hindu teachers, of course, would object to the title Non-realism, since for the Vedanta the Real is the deep inner world of the psyche and the Unreal (Maya) is the world we perceive through our senses. The dreaming world represented an intermediate 'reality'. The famous Upanishadic prayer, "Lead me from the UnReal to the Real," means 'from my deluded obsession with the overt world towards my own depths'.

Bill, a friend of mine, believed he had died. When he suffered what he called his 'nervous breakdown' Bill had endured convulsions and severe pains in his head. After this experience he no longer cared whether the sun shone or it rained. He appeared to have lost his feelings, so that he no longer felt sad or happy or loving towards his family. He had no interest in anything, even hobbies that had absorbed him no longer roused one breath of enthusiasm. He gave up washing himself and shaving and sat in the window seat of his home, looking across the valley with an empty stare.
He was in this condition, he argued, because at the time of his 'nervous

breakdown' the tension in his head had actually smashed his brain, so that he was really dead. By some strange quirk of fate, he was still walking about and had not departed to the place where dead people go. Bill believed he was a zombie - one of the living dead. A psychiatrist interviewed him at a clinic and asked Bill whether dead men would bleed. Bill said, "No, dead men will not bleed."

The psychiatrist pricked Bill's thumb and drops of blood appeared on his skin. "Q.E.D." said the psychiatrist, "You are alive."

Bill thought for a moment: "Dead men must bleed, after all," he said.

Bill's language was meaningless to the modernist psychiatrist, who occupied a different linguistic space and was playing a realist language game and was not into Deconstruction. Bill's language was simply further evidence of Bill's derangement, of his schizophrenia. But if we treat the language as symbol, as a Non-Real expression of Bill's inner condition, it is perfectly meaningful within the psychological system, for instance, of Saint Paul, who taught we could be 'dead within the law'. Indeed, Paul also believed he had, himself, died and been resurrected within this life. Bill, unhappily, had not yet come through the 'tomb' to those experiences of personal transformation understood, allegorically, as 'resurrection'. He had died to his 'self', but remained in a kind of limbo, waiting to be 'born again', waiting to discover his new, unconsciously latent 'self'. Within Paul's Non-Real language game, Bill had died to his 'old Adam', but not yet discovered the mystery of the 'new Adam'.

Does not the application of the old, symbolical language of religion, the allegorical method, to the experiences of Helen and Bill make both the language and the experiences more meaningful and alive? Let us apply the method to the New Testament texts, deconstructing the metaphors:

In chapter thirteen of his Gospel, Matthew puts these words into the mouth of Jesus: "The Kingdom of Heaven is like a net thrown into the sea, which gathered fish of every kind". Matthew adds that the good fish are kept and the bad fish thrown away, maintaining the theme of the chapter (against the 'post-modern' universalists), that only the 'good' will inherit the kingdom. The saying is elaborated by Luke in Chapter Five of his Gospel into a story set at the beginning of the ministry of Jesus, where he addressed a crowd of people by the Lake of Gennesaret. There were two boats by the lake and the fishermen, who were washing their nets, had failed to catch any fish. Jesus stood in one of the boats and taught from it, a little distance from land. He then told Peter to drop his nets into the water. Peter protests, but obeys and takes in a great shoal of fish, so that the nets are breaking and the boats beginning to sink. John (or possibly an interpolator according to some scholars) relates the tale yet again in the last chapter of the Fourth Gospel; placing it at the end of the ministry, as one of the Resurrection stories.

In the Johannine account the Sea has become Tiberius and the crowd has disappeared. Jesus is on the beach and not in the boat. He calls to them to drop their nets. John is specific about the number of fish caught - one hunded and fifty three. Again there is the emphasis that the net is not torn by the weight of fish. Jesus has already made a charcoal fire and there is fish cooking and bread ready to eat. They share a meal with him.

The number of species of fish recognised in the first century was one hundred and fifty three. The number represents ALL fishes, fish of 'every kind': "I will draw all souls unto me". All people will be gathered into the Great Fisher's net; the Net, now a metaphor for the Church, will hold all sorts and conditions of people and not let them fall away. Christ will nourish and feed us all. In this account the universalists have clearly won through. The fish was a symbol of the human soul - as it was also in Hindu and Egyptian religion. The Gnostics represented Christ as the Great Fish. Through this identification the fish became associated with the Eucharist, appearing as a design on early eucharistic bowls for wine and bread. Tertullian in a work on Baptism refers to neophytes as 'little fishes'. And, of course, it provided the Christians with the famous anagram of 'Ichthus' - and a secret sign.

There are four ways to interpret a story like this: 1 Reject it entirely as incredible (as a positivist); 2. Believe it entirely, as a miracle (as a fundamentalist); 3. rationalise it by suggesting Jesus could see a shoal of fish by the boat, which the fishermen could not see - as, indeed, on some coasts a man is appointed to stand on a cliff and point out to the fishing boats where, from his vantage point, he can see shoals of fish moving in the waters (as a modernist rational empiricist); 4. use the old allegorical method of the Pharisees and Gnostics, and approach the material in a Non-Realistic (postmodern) way and interpret it as one would a myth, a poem or a dream.

The miracle, surely, is not that Jesus made a heavy catch of 153 fish two thousand years ago, but that the spiritual food we need for our inner nourishment as persons, is freely available from the depths of our natures (represented by the sea) to everyone without distinction - that we have, in what today we would call the Unconscious, astonishing depths, alive with all we need to sustain us. The Christa, the archetype of our enormous potentiality as children of the Eternal God, will draw us all into her vast net.

Amongst the gravest causes of offence by the Non-Realists within the Church of England has been their attitude towards the Resurrection. The Resurrection is not, said David Jenkins, 'a conjuring trick with old bones'. He would agree, it seems, with Harry Williams, in *True Resurrection* (4), that banishing resurrection to past and future "saves us from a lot of reality and delivers us from a great deal of fear. It has, in short, the advantage of safeguarding us from life."

The concept of the Resurrection has a long history. The Mystery Religions, which spread rapidly throughout the Roman Empire before the birth of Christianity, were frequently a syncretism of Egyptian, Zoroastrian and Greek religious ideas and practices. A shared Resurrection was at the heart of the 'mystery' - a dying and a rising again. The regenerative expectations of the devotees of the mystery religions and the popular belief in the 'resurrection' or 'immortality' of the emperor - that is, the perpetuation after death of his alter ego, his Genius - prepared the ground for Christian teaching about the resurrection of Jesus.

Zoroaster (800 BC) had taught a corporeal resurrection in which adults would live after death in bodies appearing to be forty years old. Those who had died when they were children would have resurrected bodies with the appearance of fifteen year olds. Augustine taught the resurrected bodies of Christians would correspond also to these ages and, moreover, physically and mentally handicapped people would have perfect health and form in their resurrected bodies. Zoroaster believed there would be a final judgment of the dead.

The Pharisees, by the time of Paul, had come to believe in the resurrection of the psycho-physical unity of the person and this view was adopted by many Christians. At the Second Coming of Christ the decomposed bodies of the dead would be reconstituted and their souls would re-enter them for the Final Judgment. Islam has, similarly, a teaching of a Last Judgment, involving the resurrection of the dead and the vindication of the faithful, who will be rewarded by entry into Paradise. Christianity and Islam in their official or 'orthodox' (pre-modernist and modernist) teaching eventually followed Zoroaster in declaring the wicked would face eternal damnation.

In the New Testament, however, the concept of Resurrection takes four different forms. Firstly there are the descriptions of the so-called resurrection appearances of Jesus in the Upper Room and on the Road to Emmaus - reading like the kinds of spiritual or ghostly experiences people still have, for example, during bereavement, when they hallucinate about or have visions of their lost loved ones; or like the 'appearances' of Our Lady in the hallucinations or visions of teenagers in Medjugorje, Yugoslavia, in recent years. These experiences of the Risen Christ were linked via the symbol of the empty tomb to the idea of the second form of resurrection, the Ascension of Jesus as the Christ to the Right Hand of God.

Paul preaches the Risen Christ, with Whom he believed he had communicated on the Road to Damascus. But, for Paul, the symbol of the Risen Christ becomes a living, archetypal power within his own mind. He converses with the Christ, Who has become the symbol now of the whole Body of the Church, where all believers are members one of another. Paul's position is reminiscent of the Chinese Taoist teaching (fm Lu-shih Ch'un Ch'ui):

> Heaven and Earth and all things are like the body of one person, and this is what is called the Great Unity.

This is the third form taken by the concept of the resurrection in the New Testament - resurrection as a here and now experience. Resurrection is a sharing in spiritual rebirth, renewal or regeneration, here and now - in the manner taught by the mystery religions: Eternal Life is here and now, as Jesus said. This concept of resurrection - as a symbol of transformation - was the only form of resurrection many Christians believed, including the Gnostics and some of the congregation at Corinth. Paul felt he had been initiated into this aspect of Resurrection through his experience on the Road to Damascus and that his subsequent life had been a development out of that experience.

Fourthly there was the concept of the Resurrection as a renewing of the physical body after death in preparation for Judgment. Paul's theology is not easy to assess in this matter. He does not, for example, use the word *sarx* for the resurrected 'body'. Indeed he declares emphatically that *sarx* - i.e. flesh and blood - shall not inherit the Kingdom of God. In Paul's writings *sarx* means "flesh under the law" - flesh as *nomos* ('flesh' imprisoned in modernist language games; i.e., in the jargon of depth psychology, as a super-ego directed 'self': the construct self which emerges out of the Ego-Super Ego liaison). The Greek word Paul uses to denote the resurrected 'body' is *soma* - meaning the imminded body or the 'person' - and he speaks of one's 'spiritual body' (*soma pneumatikon*).

Paul's concept of the 'spiritual body' appears to refer to the 'body' we all possess in our dreams and with which other people - dead or alive - may be clothed in our dreams and visions. The body we have in our dreams appears as complete as the body we relate to when we are awake. It may feel pain, cold and heat, hear sounds and see colours. Other people appear vividly and corporeally in our dreams and visions so we may hold them or speak with them as the disciples did with Jesus after his death and as Paul did with Jesus on the Road to Damascus. It makes sense of Paul's use of the concept of a 'spiritual body' to consider he is talking about the 'flesh and blood image bodies' of that profound and poetic imagination, which lies behind the creation of our dreams and visions.

Paul's use of the word *'soma'* is sometimes reminiscent also of the Roman concept of the Genius, inasmuch as he appears to refer to a kind of alter ego, an inner potentiality within us - there is the old Adam and the new Adam, the old person 'under the Law' and the new person 'in Christ'. The image of the Christ is a kind of inner Genius, representing our potentiality as children of God. Through this inner image of the Christ we may be transformed and renewed, and grow towards the goal, the prize of the high-calling of God, represented by the image of the Christ. *Soma* may, therefore, exist in an alienated and impoverished condition - 'under the Law' and 'in sin' - or it may exist in a liberated and maturing condition - 'in Christ'. In this latter condition, the person shares that glorious liberty represented by the resurrection as a transformational symbol: to be 'in Christ' is to share already in the resurrection.

Resurrection is described by Paul as an arousal or an awakening. Resurrection is a being 'raised' - *egeiro* - which means to be raised up, but also to awaken. Resurrection is also *anastasis*, a standing up beyond one's self, a rising again. Resurrection involves an awakening and an arousal from one's old self, transformative of the person in relation both to one's self and to others. The act of surrender, of trusting commitment - faith - permits this transformation to occur, a transformation restoring (*dikaios* - tr. 'righteousness'; basic meaning 'to restore') the individual to a living relationship with the inner creative powers of the psyche, captured in the archetypal image of the Christ.

The Gnostics, condemned as heretics, believed with Origen that the resurrection was not a past event, unique to Jesus of Nazareth, which might be shared at the second coming, but that it symbolised an awakening now to the presence of the Christ in the soul. The anonymous Gnostic text, *Treatise on Resurrection,* addressed to Rheginos, explains that ordinary human existence is a form of spiritual death, but that resurrection is the moment of enlightenment: "It is ... the revealing of what truly exists ... and a transition (*metabole*) into newness." One may, he declares, be resurrected from the dead here and now.

In Buddhism there is the teaching that the Buddha had three bodies, the third of which is a 'resurrection' body. The first body was the flesh-and-blood body (*nirmananakaya*) of Siddhartha, corresponding to the human body of Jesus; a second body of the Buddha (*dharmakaya*) is eternal and wholly beyond sense perception, corresponding to the notion of Christ as the unchanging Child of God, coeternal with God; and thirdly, the 'enjoyment body' (bringing peace and joy) of the Buddha (*sambhogakaya*), which lies somewhere between the human and the divine, appears to individual Buddhists to aid and encourage their quest for nirvana.

OLIVER SACKS

Let us digress to consider a practical example of Non-Realistic Resurrection - press a little further towards the Deconstruction of this theological metaphor: In 1966 Oliver Sacks, an Englishman trained as a neurologist, entered the wards of Mount Carmel Hospital, New York, where he met patients who had been in the hospital since the great epidemic of encephalitis lethargica (sleeping sickness) just after the First World War. Described as 'extinct volcanoes' by Von Economo, who first elaborated the condition in the 19th Century, they erupted into life in 1969, in a manner he could not have imagined. The hitherto placid atmosphere of Mount Carmel was transformed by the dramatic 'awakening' or 'quickening' of 80 or more of these patients, who were regarded and regarded themselves as effectively 'dead'.

It was not a purely 'medical' excitement that swept the hospital, wrote Sacks, but a tremendous 'human' excitement at seeing the 'dead' awaken again - like a resurrection (hence the title of his book, *Awakenings*(5) from Ibsen's 'When We Dead Awaken'). Because of the long term relationships in that hospital between patients and staff, it was impossible for the staff to think of their patients as 'cases' or 'statistics' - but only as individuals. Their transformation from near cadaverous or corpse-like existence was deeply moving to everyone.

In the 1950s it had been established that the brain of people suffering Parkinson's disease (described by Parkinson in London, 1817) lacked a transmitter called dopamine and it was believed it might be 'normalised' if the level of dopamine could be raised. But attempts to do this with L-Dopa (precursor of dopamine) in milligram quantities, failed persistently - until through a mighty act of imagination and audacity George Cotzias gave a group of patients L-Dopa in doses of a thousand times greater than had ever been used. The outlook for Parkinsonian patients was changed - a sudden, unbelievable hope appeared.

Sacks and colleagues tried the drug on their patients with astonishing results. They were equally audacious. Ninety days was the official limit of use; but taking his patients off the drug seemed like committing them back to death. He used it on 60 patients for a whole year.

In 1970 he reported to the Journal of the American Medical Association his findings: how all had done well at first, but all of them, sooner or later, had "escaped from control, had entered complex, sometimes bizarre, and unpredictable states"; which he found himself unable to conceive as 'side-effects', but regarded as integral parts of an evolving whole. Ordinary policies ceased to work - there was need for a deeper, more radical understanding of what was going on. His report met great opposition, disbelief and denial - so much so he believed he must be up against something extremely important, beyond the treatment of the patients, which, in the end, he could understand and express only by using existentialist and religious language and concepts. In discussing, for example, the way in which healing occurs he says: "Our deepest and most mysterious strengths are called forth from the depths of our being, about which we know so little."

Charcot had described the affinities between depression, catatonia, hysteria and Parkinsonism in the eighteen sixties and believed Parkinsonism was not merely a disease or syndrome of symptoms, but "a strange form of behaviour; a peculiar and characteristic mode of Being-in-the-World". Charcot described the symptoms as "the final, futile outcome of inner strugggles and the draining of energy in futile inner battles" - as if his patients were somehow divided within themselves, a will and counter will; a civil war of the mind.

Sacks' patients experienced what he and they described as 'resurrection', however temporary or spasmodic these experiences might be, when this inner conflict of will suddenly ceased. As if the 'war in their members', to use a phrase from Paul, had been resolved and they were free for a while from the extraordinary inner tensions out of which the symptoms arose. It was as if Peter's angel had broken their inner chains and smashed the prison walls.

Resurrection represents a transformation of consciousness arising out of deep suffering, a kind of Crucifixion of spirit. The patients at Mount Carmel, who had in some sense 'died', now had 'Awakened' into life. The role of Love in this transformation engaged Sacks' intelligence - the love which grew between patients and staff, allowing these patients to feel 'at home' in their situation. Transformation and its perpetuation in their lives seemed to him intimately related to their developing ability to love themselves and their world. It was as if the drug provided a key that unlocked new possibilities; or an explosive that temporarily undermined the foundations of their interior prisons. But, whether a satisfactory and fruitful healing of the person took place in the long term - and however fitfully - lay ultimately beyond anything the drug might do and could not be achieved through 'drug dependance'. It arose wherever the patients were able, in consequence of their 'awakenings', to discover within their relationships with each other, the staff and the world beyond them, the miraculous joys and healing power of love - learning painfully how to love and how to accept love. Sacks wrote:

> One sees that beautiful and ultimate metaphysical truth, which has been stated by poets and physicians and metaphysicians in all ages - by Leibniz and Donne and Dante and Freud: that Eros is the oldest and strongest of the gods; that Love is the alpha and omega of being; and that the work of healing, of rendering whole, is, first and last, the business of Love.

THE GNOSTICS AND RESURRECTION

Theodotus (6), a second century Gnostic teacher in Asia Minor, wrote a Gnostic was one who had come to understand:

> who we were, and what we have become; where we were ... whither we are hastening; from what we are being released; what birth is and what is rebirth.

To know one's self, at the very deepest level of our inner being, was, simultaneously, to know God - this was the secret of Gnosis.

One of the greatest of the Gnostic poets, Monoimus (7), wrote:

> Abandon search for God and the creation and other matters of a similar sort. Look for God by taking yourself as the starting point. Learn who it is within you who makes everything his own and says: 'My God, my mind, my thought, my soul, my body' Learn the sources of sorrow, joy, love, hate ... If you carefully investigate these matters you will find God in yourself.

According to the Gnostic *Gospel of Thomas* (8) Jesus declared he was not the Master of his disciples, but that they could follow where he trod and know, in their own experience, the things he had discovered. In this Gospel Jesus ridicules those who thought of the Kingdom of God in literal, Realist terms:

> Rather, the Kingdom is inside of you, and it is outside of you. When you come to know yourselves, then you will be known, and you will realise that you are the children of the living God. But if you will not know yourselves, then you dwell in poverty, and it is you who are that poverty.

Like teachers of prayer the world over, and like the modern depth psychologists, the Gnostic teachers saw the integration or maturation of the personality, the transformation of the soul, as a process depending upon our co-operation with inner, or unconscious, healing powers, associated with the work of the Holy Spirit and known as 'the life of Grace' in Christian contemplative theology.

The Christians in authority within the early church believed Jesus was the Son of God in a unique way, quite distinct from any other human being; a specially selected God/Man, whose sacrifice on the Cross atoned for human sin - i.e. bought back our souls (redeemed us) from the Devil. The Gnostics, however, emphasised the common humanity of Jesus. They believed the Christ is incarnate in every human being. Jesus was one who became the Christ; "was filled with the Holy Spirit", realising within himself the implications of the Christ as incarnate Logos - that inner Light which enlightens the souls of all folk everywhere.

The Buddhist scholar, Edward Conze, believed the Gnostics were influenced by Buddhist teaching. Buddhists teach that the 'Diamond Body of the Buddha' indwells every human soul, just as classical Christian teachers, such as Saint Augustine, believed the God or Christ image - representing the totality of our human and divine potentiality - lay at the fundus of every human soul. Augustine called this indwelling 'image' an archetype (meaning imprinted from the beginning). It is a fascinating parallel in the History of Ideas that the modern depth psychologist, Carl.G. Jung, used this same term 'archetype' of images appearing in dreams and visions, representing inherited human psychobiological potential. The image of the Christ or the Buddha, Jung believed, represented the inner Self, centre of unconsciousness, from which deep integrative or healing processes within the mind were derived.

The very early church appears to have enjoyed a rich variety of theological position, but by AD 200 Christianity had become a hierarchical institution of bishops, priests and deacons, who believed themselves guardians of the one and only true faith. What constituted the one and only true faith was, ironically, decided by majority vote and rejected viewpoints were then persecuted as heresies.

Gnosticism existed before Christianity, as a religion in its own right. Its roots were in the Mystery Religions of the Middle East and in Zoroastrianism. There was exchange and fusion between Christians and Gnostics until a form of Christian Gnosticism emerged producing its own gospels and richly symbolical poetic texts; it has been said of them, that they rationalised mythology. Freud and Jung, in the twentieth century, also taught us to rationalise mythology, restoring to us the wonderful psychological dramas of the human soul captured in mythology, by teaching us not to treat them literally, but as a form of universal dream, a rich dynamic representation of the inner world of the psyche and its struggles and vicissitudes. The interpretation of dreams, visions and myths requires a subtle interplay of reason and intuition.

Not only did the Gnostics emphasise the priority of the authority of experience, of the Spirit working in the human mind rather than external authorities of prelate or text or dogma, they also did not believe literally in the New Testament narrative. Rather, they followed the old pharisaic method of interpreting scripture allegorically, recognising, for example, that the Christmas stories of the Virgin Birth, the Singing Angels, the Star and the Wise Men; and the Resurrection narrative, too, should be interpreted as myth or poetry.

It is true there were many Gnostic sects and differing teachings amongst them, as there were amongst the early Christians, and some teachings would certainly not appeal to most moderns, such as the sharp dualism claimed by many Gnostics between an evil world created by a Satanic demiurge and possible salvation through union with a good God; or the belief, maintained by some Gnostics, that Jesus did not have a real, fleshly body and, therefore, could not suffer.

NON-REALISM

Believing the incarnation is true universally of human souls and that Jesus is not uniquely the Child of God, but that we are all children of God, a Postmodernist Non-Realism allows us to view other religious leaders without condescension, to recognise Jesus of Nazareth as a great religious poet and teacher, but also able to recognise the authority of other truly outstanding religious poets and teachers such as Siddhartha Gautama, the Buddha, and the Taoist sage, Lao Tzu. Non-Realists may read the scriptures of other faiths, their poetry and teaching stories, as readily as the Bible - not as somewhat secondary or inferior writings, but as valid and significant in their own right. This makes for a genuine tolerance and understanding of other religious traditions, providing a milieu in which we may meet and engage with people of different faiths as equals, as sisters and brothers in search of truth; and not as rivals.

Christian theologians struggled to make meaning of the life and death of Jesus in ways that would allow them to identify Jesus with the concepts of the Christ and the Logos. How could they reconcile the presence of the human and the divine·in one person? What emerged from this intellectual conflict was not one doctrine of the Trinity, but many - the doctrine of the Trinity by Sabellius, the one by Origen, the one by Irenaeus, the one by Tertullian, the one by Nestorius, the one by Eusebius, the one by Arius and so on. It was Constantine who brought the whole debate into focus at the Council of Nicaea in Bythnia in the summer of 325 AD. He insisted the three hundred bishops attending at Nicaea should reach unanimity, or at least a majority concensus on the Trinity.

Four vital issues arose out of the decision at Nicaea. Firstly, from now on the unity of the church is identical with the majority of the bishops. Christianity is no longer a democratic movement. Secondly, Arius and his followers are banned and persecuted. The bishops now decide what is and what is not the one true faith and may pursue to the death anyone who speaks out against their concensus. Thirdly, the church has become a state church; religion and politics are now inextricably intertwined. Fourthly, Jesus emerges as God and Man - a man who became God; in some sense at one with God. Jesus avoids the fate of becoming a half-god, a god like the gods of Olympus. His divinity belongs to his nature. At the same time, however, Jesus is identified with the Christ (i.e. with the Son/Child, the Logos), in a way that appears to make him totally, uniquely different from any other human being.

A core implication of Non-Realism is that the concepts and language of religion do not refer to events whose fruition and ultimate significance lies beyond death, but refer rather to this life - to the here and now. Cultural training does not prepare us for thinking of our personal development as a process - as a movement from death to life, rather than from life to death; as a sleep from which we need to awaken. How, apart from miracle and sign, may we understand the declaration of Jesus at the beginning of his ministry, that he had come to bind up the broken-hearted, to proclaim liberty to those who are captive, to open the prison for those who are bound?   How indeed may the blind see, the deaf hear, those who are dead be returned to life?   'Realism' offers such an appealing and attractive option.   It is so much easier to accept the whole thing, miracles and all; or to reject the whole thing, miracles and all and take on a comfortable atheism (as opposed to the convoluted via negativa of 'non-theism'); or to rationalise the myths into the impotence of empirical common sense, than it is to rationalise the myths by interpretation and follow the Path where the allegory, smiling darkly, points us on the Way.

A Non-Real understanding of the Resurrection invites us to consider that personal transformation, awakening, is a Real and ever present possibility. We cannot, however, 'awaken' by conscious choice, but contingently through struggle and grief, a crucifixion of spirit and an acknowledgment of our entombment. As Harry Williams wrote in *True Resurrection (9)*, "the prelude to resurrection as we experience it in this life is always powerlessness." The transformation process surges mysteriously, unaccountably, mercifully, from our own depths, as we lend ourselves to it - from the Potentia which, though in some respects unique, we each share with everyone - as we discover the astonishing miracle of love; learn painfully and with much conflict the joy of loving and being loved.

Here lies the essential nature of resurrection as a restoration after 'darkness' and 'entombment'.   The paradigm of the life of Jesus is a spiritual paradigm applicable to the spiritual path, the path of personal renewal.   Crucifixion of spirit, the entombment of dark despair and unknowing are the prelude to renewal; as the descent into hell appears a necessary prerequisite for the ascent into heaven.   The descent into hell is the fall towards the Abyss which makes us aware of our walled-in-ness, *circumvallatus* as Luther put it - the original meaning of the Anglo-Saxon word 'hell' - to fence or wall in.

A deconstruction of the expression 'damned to hell' may make this discussion simpler to follow.   Hell means 'to be held in', fenced in, repressed even. Damnation means 'to be doomed'; which is 'to be determined' in the sense, say, of being 'determined' by our genes, 'determined' or 'conditioned' by our environment, our culture and childhood training. We are doomed to alienation or spiritual imprisonment (soul death).   'Resurrection' captures the possibility of becoming free from our inner prisons, of arising from the bed upon which we sleep as we are bound.   'Saviours' are those who liberate us, whose example, teaching, work, illuminates us and sets us free.   Jesus and Socrates and the Buddha are amongst the greatest liberators, saviours, of humanity; but all artists, philosophers and poets true to their Core, are also saviours and liberators - including Mozart and Beethoven, Van Gogh and Picasso, to name but a few of the exceptionally gifted liberators of humanity, to whom we are indebted.

The descent into 'hell' (a recognition of one's encapsulated condition) always precedes the ascent into 'heaven'. Heaven represents the sense of openness and freedom, of restoration, which follows our resignation to the prison-house of the soul in which we have lived, unconscious of the severity of its restrictions. One sees elderly folk fall into the deep depression and angst they have managed to fight off all their lives, now that age and infirmity has weakened their defences. One sees, again, how this is the razor's edge. Some fall into unmanageable states of deep clinical depression, but others work through their regression into infantilism to new levels of integrative living - of serenity and joy.

DYING TO DEATH

Bill, whom I referred to earlier in this chapter as the man who believed he was a zombie, one of the living dead, was a continuous source of inspiration to me. He appeared to capture, symbolise in his evident pathology, spiritual truth ordinarily hidden in us by our adaptive defences; the truth expressed in the Pauline concept of 'being dead within the law'. Bill's internal aridity took all flavour from his living. He sat day after day, looking through his kitchen window at the garden beyond, never caring to wash or shave; unmoved by sun or rain.

He had had no sexual relationships in his life, until he joined the navy. Bill had been so uncomfortable in the presence of women he would not go into a shop where there was a woman serving behind the counter. On shore leave in the Navy he went, on impulse, to a brothel with other sailors and had sexual intercourse with a prostitute. He enjoyed the experience, but was filled with a guilt greatly exacerbated by news the same week of the death of his mother. He returned home on compassionate leave and had the 'nervous breakdown' which he believed had destroyed his brain. Occasionally he would masturbate, phantasising about the prostitute, but then be overwhelmed once more by guilt, assuming the death of his mother and the destruction of his brain were a punishment for his sin in sleeping with the prostitute.

Shortly after I began work with him he had the sudden suspicion that perhaps his condition was caused by syphilis contracted from the prostitute and he attended a sex clinic for tests, which revealed he had not been infected with syphilis. He then admitted he heard voices speaking in his head, whose messages, reluctantly, he repeated to me; voices saying obscene and sharply critical things about him. Gradually he recognised these voices as the voices of members of his family, including his mother and father. Throughout his childhood and youth, he felt, his family had conveyed that sex was dirty and forbidden and dangerous and that he, himself, was dirty, of little worth, unless he behaved within the narrow mores they taught him. "I felt that if I did not comply, something really dreadful would happen to me."

Watching Bill deconstruct this conditioning over several years and gradually gain an independent set of values, slowly discovering a sense of worth and meaning in his life, was a moving experience. He began, eventually, to take up interests he had long abandoned, including painting and music and a passion for motor cars, and to make relationships with men and women. It was like watching someone unfold, as in the case of the people described in Kahn's book, *When The Spring Comes*, or the patients at Mount Carmel Hospital where Sacks worked, Bill felt he had been raised from the dead, as if he had been resurrected here and now.

The Muslim poet, Rumi,(10) describes resurrection as an event we may experience many times. Muhammed, he says, is one who has experienced resurrection again and again and again. Just as the Zen teachers speak of little satori and big satori so there are little resurrections and big resurrections. There are gentle transformations, changing our attitude to this or that, and there are disturbing transformations, which bring us into deep conflict and shift our whole sense of who we are and of how we perceive our world.

I.M. Lewis in *Ecstatic Religion*(10) describes the shaman as one who dies and is reborn many times. The shaman's initiatory experience "is represented as an involuntary surrender to disorder, as he is thrust protesting into the chaos which the ordered and controlled life of society strives so hard to deny." Like Saint Paul, the shaman dies daily: "Out of the agony of affliction and the dark night of the soul comes literally the ecstasy of spiritual victory."

A significant role for deviance lies in its ability to break us from the prison-house of normality; to wrench us from our sleep in the boxed-in-world of hell towards a new awakening to our existential condition. It represents a move from the Right Hand of acceptable respectability to the Left Hand Path of nonconformity, dissent and stigma, in the hope eventually, the Buddhists say, of finding the way to the Middle Path of spiritual growth and integrity that lies between them. Our extremity, says the ancient tag, is God's opportunity. Deviance makes it difficult for us to rest securely in the obscurantism of normality. It challenges self-satisfaction and self-righteousness and allows expression to the great and desperate cry of the Lost Child; it gives voice to those who are oppressed, it gives tangible form to disquiet and discontent, it represents a cry for help hidden in dark and, sometimes, dreadfully destructive deeds - in the violence, for example, of crimes against the person.

The response of the Moral Right down the centuries, of course, has been to express their own unconscious sadism even more violently against offenders in brutal reprisals and cruel laws. The attempt to understand is interpreted as an attempt to excuse and those who defend the deviant and oppressed minorities find themselves sharing their fate, like Christ sharing the penalty imposed on his companions in agony - the two thieves.

That which a society describes as deviancy at once reveals and defines the pathology of the whole community from which it has arisen and against which it now offends. Like the leper's bell, our so-called deviancies toll the hollow peal of our cultural disorder, continuously reminding the community of the presence of what we dread and would like to ignore. When the Puritans unmercifully persecuted adulterers with cruel tar and feathers and branded their foreheads with a scarlet letter, they revealed both their terror at what they perceived as a serious threat to their precariously narrow world and also a vicious rage that their desperate attempts to eradicate its challenge from their midst were clearly unsuccessful. The scarlet letter, whilst excommunicating the adulterer, nonetheless continuously announced to the whole world, in an ironic paradox, the abject failure of the Puritan regime, for all its narrow harshness, to order and control its communities. From this kind of intolerant and savage confrontation the condemned deviant will always, in historic time, emerge triumphant, since he or she wins sympathy and compassion as the victim of an inhumane persecution.

Those who take the stance of the Moral Right are, of course, despite protestations to the contrary, not truly into understanding or compassion, impeded as they are by a determination to resist any invitations from either Eros or Agape. And the followers of the Moral Right find, in their taking upon themselves the role of judge, they are themselves judged both in a higher court and by posterity.

Descent into the knowledge of the prison-house of our adaptability, the sense of that pathology which conjoins us, however unconsciously, with the deviant in society, will bring us into touch with our own internal chaos. But we do not tread the depths alone, since the Form of the Fourth will divide the great waters and make a path for us, so we may travel through the wilderness towards the promise of a resurrection, a transformed relation with ourselves and our world.

Resurrection may come as a rising into an experience where words fall away from things and there is a vital sense of the 'isness' of everything: a no-thing-ness for which we cannot find words to express. A grand resurrection may be like the first, amazing falling in love of a couple leading through agonies of conflict and disillusionment, projection and regression, to something gradually enriched in time as the partners grow in love: grow in love in such a way that we recognise their union as a truly appropriate symbol for one's ultimate union - the eternal *unio coniunctionis*, the spiritual marriage of the soul with its own depths.

We live in the kind of universe, now, where anything seems possible - even life after death. The Resurrection, in Non-Real terms, however, represents a transformation whereby we may cease looking for new ways of clinging to our sense of self in this or any other life and, rather, die to self in that self-effacement out of which profound love for others arises, bringing us to a perplexing paradox: that true resurrection is found in the very renunciation of the desire for resurrection.

And the concept of 'THE' Resurection, the hope of a Resurrection to include the whole of humanity, would then surely correspond to what Teilhard de Chardin referred to as the Omega point in time when all the cultures and societies of the world had suffered such transformation of consciousness that we might, hopefully, astonishingly, come at last to the place where the Common wealth of God was freely available and evident in our world; to the place where the ancient angelic and prophetic visions of peace and goodwill on earth, of the lion lying with the lamb, were finally realised, bringing past and present into a new and glorious harmony, an all-inclusive *jouissance* of cosmic proportions:

The sucking child shall play over the hole of the asp,
and the weaned child shall put his hand in the adder's den.
They shall not hurt or destroy in all my holy mountain;
for the earth shall be full of the knowledge of God
as the waters cover the sea.

Isaiah 11.

NOTES TO CHAPTER SIX

1. Jean Paul Sartre. *Nausea.* Penguin Books.1969. Pp.182/3

2. Jacob Boehme. *Confessions.* Methuen. 1954. P.18
3. Hermann Hesse. *Siddhartha.* Picador. 1974. P.113

4. Harry A. Williams. *True Resurrection.* Beazley.1972.
5. Oliver Sacks. *Awakenings.* Picador. 1990 ed.

6. Elaine Pagels. *The Gnostic Gospels.* Weidenfeld and Nicolson. 1979. P. XIX.

7. Pagels. Ibid. P.XX.

8. Robert M. Grant and David Noel Freedman. *The Secret Sayings of Jesus.* *Fontana.* 1960.   P.115

9. Harry A. Williams. Ibid. P. 175.

10. *Rumi.* tr. Reynold A. Nicholson. Allen & Unwin. 1973. P.131.

11. I.M. Lewis. *Ecstastic Religion.* Penguin. 1971. P. 188
    page 121

BIBLIOGRAPHY

Maggy Anthony. *The Valkyries: The Women Around Jung.* Element Books. 1990.

Augustine. tr. Burnaby, J. *Augustine: Later Works.*SCM.1955.

Beck, U. and Beck-Gernsheim, E. *The Normal Chaos of Love..* Tr. Mark Ritter and Jane Wibel. Polity Press. 1995

Martin S. Bergmann. *Anatomy of Loving.* Columbia. 1987.

Philippa Berry and Andrew Wernick. *Shadow of Spirit.* Routledge.1992.

Mario Biagioli. *Galileo,* Courtier. Chicago. 1994.

Robert Bly. *Iron John.* Element Books. 1990.

Jacob Boehme. *Confessions.* Methuen. 1954.

Boyarin, D. *Carnal Israel.* California Univ. Press. 1993.

Judith Butler. *Bodies That Matter.* Routledge. 1993.

Cassirer, E., *Language and Myth*, tr. Langer, S.K. Dover Books. 1953.

Lionel Casson. *Ancient Egypt.* Time-Life International. 1966.

Chasseguet-Smirgel, J. *Creativity and Perversion.* New York. IUP. 1978.

Chodorow,N. *Femininities, Masculinities, Sexualities: Freud and Beyond.* Free Association. 1994.

Coward, H. *Derrida and Indian Philosophy.* Sri Satguru Publications. 1991.

Derrida, J. *Writing and Difference* tr. Bass,A. Routledge. 1990 ed. The Gift Of Death. tr. Willis,D. Chicago. 1995.

David C. Doel. *The Perennial Psychology.* Lindsey Press. 1990
That Glorious Liberty. Lindsey Press. 1994.
Out of Clouds and Darkness.. Lindsey Press. 1992.

Laura Esquirol. *Like Water For Chocolate.* Black Swan Books. 1994.

O. Fenichel *Collected Papers*, I, 167 - 180. W.W. Norton. 1953.

The *Clinical Diary of Sandor Ferenczi.* ed. Judith Dupont. tr. Michael Balint and Nicola Zarday Jackson. Harvard. 1988.

Finn, Geraldine. *The Politics of Spirituality*, fm *Shadow of Spirit*, ed. Berry & Warnick. Routledge. 1992.
George Frankl. *Archaeology of the Mind.* Open Gate Press. 1990. Vol. 1.

Sigmund Freud. *On Sexuality* Vol. 7. Pelican Freud Library. Penguin.1979. and *Collected Papers.* Hogarth. tr. Baines, C.M. 1957 ed.

Erich Fromm. *The Art Of Loving.* Allen and Unwin. 1957.

Ed.Pamela Church Gibson and Roma Gibson. *Dirty Looks.* British Film Institute Publishing. 1993.

Rosemary Goring. *From The Living Rock-Face.* New Times Press. 1995.

Robert M. Grant and David Noel Freedman. *The Secret Sayings of Jesus.* Fontana. 1960.

Muriel Green and Anne Townsend. *Hidden Treasure. Darton,* Longman and Todd. 1994.

Robert B. Greenblatt. *Love Lives of the Famous.* MTP Press. 1978.

Gospel Of Thomas. Robert M. Grant and David Noel Freedman. Fontana Books. 1960.

Guntrip, H. *Schizoid Penomena, Object Relations and the Self.* Hogarth.1968.

John R. Haule. *Divine Madness: Archetypes of Romantic Love.* Shambhala Pubs. 1990.

Heidegger,M. *What Is Called Thinking?*, tr. Wieck, F.D., Harper and Row. 1968. and Heidegger, M. Heidegger: *Basic Writings.* ed. Krell,D. Harper and Row. 1977. and *Being and Time.* SCM. 1962.

Hermann Hesse. *Siddhartha*. Picador. 1974.

Hobson, R. *Forms of Feeling*. Tavistock. 1985.

Steve Humphries and Pamela Gordon. *Forbidden Britain*. BBC Books. 1994.

Luce Irigaray. 'He Risks Who Risks Life Itself', tr. David Macey, fm. *The Irigaray Reader*. ed. Margaret Whitford. Blackwell. 1991.

St. John of the Cross. tr. Peers, A. *Complete Works*, Vol. 1. Burns Oates.

Dame Julian of Norwich. *Revelations of Divine Love*.Burns Oates.1952

Jung, C.G. *Complete Works*. Vol 11. Routledge. 1958.
Memories, Reflections, Dreams. Routledge. 1963.

M.Masud R.Khan. *When Spring Comes Chatto* & Windus. 1988.
Alienation in Perversions. Karnac.1989 ed.

Louise J. Kaplan. *Female Perversions*. Penguin. 1991.

John Kerr. *A Most Dangerous Method*: The Story of Jung, Freud and Sabina Spielrein. Sinclair-Stevenson. 1994.

Soren Kierkegaard. trl. Lowrie. *The Sickness Unto Death*. Doubleday. 1954.

Kohut, H. *The Search for the Self.* N. York. Norton. 1984. *How Does Analysis Cure? Chicago*. 1984.

Julia Kristeva. *Tales of Love*. Columbia. 1987.

The *Hysterical Male*, ed. Arthur and Marie Louise Kroker. Macmillan. 1991.

Milan Kundera. *The Unbearable Lightness of Being*. tr. Heim, M.H. Faber and Faber. 1987 ed.

Lacan, J. *Ecrits*, Tavistock. 1977.
The Four Fundamental Concepts of Psycho-analysis. Penguin. 1977.

Tony Lake and Ann Hills. *Affairs.* Open Books. 1979.

Thomas Laqueur. *Making Sex.* Harvard. 1992.

Philip Larkin. *Collected Poems.* Faber and Faber. 1988.

Leary, T. *Psychedelic Experience.* Academy Editions. 1964.

I.M. Lewis. *Ecstastic Religion.* Penguin. 1971.

Martin Luther. *Letters Of Spiritual Counsel.* ed. Theodore G. Tappert. SCM. 1955.

Jean-Luc Marion. *God Without Being.* 1991 Chicago.

The Cloud of Unknowing, ed. McCann, J. with commentary by Fr. Augustine Baker. Burns Oates. 1952 ed.

Francis A. Macnab. *Estrangement And Relationship.* Tavistock. 1965.

Alice Miller. *For Your Own Good. Faber.* 1982.

Millett,K. *Sexual Politics.* Doubleday. 1969.

A.A.Milne. *The House At Pooh Corner.* Methuen. 1979.

Michel de Montaigne. *Travel Journal.* tr. Donald Frame. North Point Press. 1983.

Erich Neumann. *The Great Mother.* Princeton University Press. 1974.

Nicholson, S. *The Goddess Re-Awakening.* Quest Books. 1989.

Pagels, E. *The Gnostic Gospels.* Weidenfeld and Nicholson. 1980.

Pantel, P.S. *A History of Women.* Vol. 1. Harvard. 1992.

Perkins, M.A., *Coleridge's Philosophy.* Oxford. 1994

Person, E.S. *Love and Fateful Encounters.* Bloomsbury. 1989.

Plato. *The Republic.* tr. Cornford, F.M., Oxford. 1942.
The Letters of Abelard And Heloise. tr. Betty Radice. Penguin. 1975.
Rhadakrishnan,S. *The Bhagavadgita.*Allen & Unwin. 1963

Paul Roazen. *Freud And His Followers.* Penguin. 1979.

Aline Rousselle. *Body Politics in Ancient Rome.* Fm. A History of Women.Vol.1.
ed. P.S. Pantel. Harvard.1992.

Rumi. tr. Reynold A. Nicholson. Allen & Unwin. 1973.

Peter Rutter. *Sex In The Forbidden Zone.* Mandala. 1990.

Andrew Samuels. *The Political Psyche.* Routledge. 1993.

Oliver Sacks. *Awakenings.* Picador. 1990 ed.

Dimensions of Psychoanalysis. ed. Joseph Sandler. Karnac Books.1989.

Jean Paul Sartre. *Being and Nothingness.* Methuen. 1966 ed.

Richard Schacht. *Alienation.* Allen and Unwin. 1971.

Edward Schillebeeckx. *Jesus.* Collins. 1979.

Katsuki Sekida. *Zen Training.* Weatherhill. 1975. Pp.137 ff.

Anna Marie Smith. *New Right Discourse On Race and Sexuality.* Cambridge.
1994.

James R. and Lynn G. Smith. *Beyond Monogamy.* John Hopkins. 1974.

Alexander Solzhenitsyn.*The Gulag Archipelago.* Fontana.1974.

Sommers, C.H. *Who Stole Feminism.* Simon and Schuster. 1994.

Annie Sprinkle. *Post Porn Modernist.* Torch Books. 1991.

Robert J. Stoller. *Sex and Gender.* Karnac Books. 1984.
Observing the Erotic Imagination. Yale. 1985.

Anthony Storr. *The School of Genius.* Deutsch. 1991.

Reay Tannahill. *Sex in History.* Abacus Books.1981.

Paul Tillich. *The Shaking of the Foundations.* Pelican. 1966.

Tustin, F. *Autism and Childhood Psychosis.* Hogarth. 1972.

Lao Tzu. tr. Arthur Waley. *The Way And Its Power.* Longmans. 1956.

Wicksteed, P.H. *The Reactions Between Dogma and Philosophy* Williams and Norgate. 1920.

The Works Of Oscar Wilde. ed. John Gilbert. 1977. Cassell.

Harry A. Williams. *True Resurrection.* Beazley.1972.

Irvin D. Yalom. *Existential Psychotherapy.* Basic Books. 1990.

R.C. Zaehner. *Concordant Discord.* Oxford. 1970.

Zolla, E. *The Androgyne.* Thames and Hudson. 1981.

GLOSSARY

ABREACTION is the re-experiencing vividly, with full emotional content, of past experiences, usually from childhood and infancy.

AGORAPHOBIA is one of the classical phobias - a fear of open spaces; a clinging to the familiar and the known; a projection of the Ego's fear of losing the boundaries of its own identity or sense of self. It is the complementary phobia to claustrophobia, a projection onto the world of the Ego's dawning apprehension of its encapsulation or alienation - its imprisonment within a particular sense of identity.

ALIENATION is an arid separation from our own roots, the ground of our being; the ennui that derives from the split betwen the conscious and unconscious sides of the mind. It represents difficulty in making relationships with one's self, other and the natural world. It corresponds to the concept of SIN in contemplative literature.

ALTER EGO is our other self, our complementary inner Twin, the unconscious counterpart to the Ego.

ANIMA is the name given by Jung to the feminine principle, to the active image of femininity in the mind, represented by female figures in our dreams and containing lost, complementary, potential aspects of the self.

ANIMUS is the name given by Jung to the masculine principle, to the active image of masculinity in the mind, represented by male figures in our dreams and also containing lost, complementary and potential aspects of the self. Like Yin and Yang in ancient Chinese texts, the anima and animus represent complementary opposites within human nature. These complementary aspects have to do with our sense of gender, with the complements of passivity and activity, of intuition and reason, of nurturing and pressing for individual expression, of instinctual and socialised sides of our nature and so on.

ARCHETYPE is a term used in the writings of Augustine, later taken over by Jung, meaning something imprinted in the mind from the beginning. Archetypes make their presence felt in our dreaming world in powerful natural images such as the sea, symbol of life and the unconscious; the eagle as symbol of the flight of reason and imagination; the Mother or Father as symbols of motherhood and fatherhood and so on. The Anima and Animus are also archetypes. The God or Christ image is also an archetype. Arechetypes represent psychobiological potential inherited universally by all human beings and appearing in common images in the myths of all cultures.

ATHANASIUS was a fourth century bishop, whose credal statement was accepted by a majority vote in the Council of Nicaea in 325 AD. It is now found in the Book of Common Prayer and known as The Athanasian Creed. The Athanasian statement about the Trinity became the official line of the Christian Church and Trinitarianism became identified with holding to this creed. Anti-Trinitarianism became synonymous with the non-acceptance of the Athanasian Creed - although, of course, there were in fact several varieties of the Trinitariän formula.

AUTISM is the name given to a mental condition in which a person is caught up completely in their own phantasy world, in their own image-making. By AUTISTIC POCKET is meant the general habit amongst us, of living in our thought processes, especially in the use of words in the mind, which tends to rob us of direct perception of our world.

CASTRATION COMPLEX is an expression deriving from Freud, meaning a fear of being castrated, a threat used to make children comply and, perhaps, one root of conscience. It came to be used more fluidly by subsequent psychotherapists to refer not merely to fears of actual castration, but to the symbolical severing of the head from the body; i.e. to represent the splitting of instinct from the rational processes so that we become ill at ease with, guilty about our natural appetites, especialy our sexual appetites. An inhibition of potential.

CHARACTER ARMOUR refers to the ways in which we hold ourselves physically - our posture for example. These physical expressions of the stance we take towards life, may create areas of stress and produce psychosomatic symptoms. Harry's tendency to walk about with clenched fists, for example, was a kind of character armour that betrayed the stance of anger and determination he brought to his work. It led eventually to arthritis in his hands and shoulders.

CONTEMPLATIVE is the name given to a form of prayer, designed to still the mind, of which Yoga is an example - in particular to check the dominion of verbal images in consciousness and to put us in touch with our own depths.

DARK NIGHTS are the periods of intense struggle with despair and anxiety, with meaninglessness and hopelessness, with the loss of identity, with growing inability to take joy in the world of the senses, which people may go through in contemplative prayer and in psychotherapy and counselling.

DEMYTHOLOGISING means recognising the myths in the Biblical texts and treating them as symbolical of the life of the Spirit and our relationship with Christ, rather than as accounts of historical events. The term was especially linked with Rudolf Bultmann, but the 'allegorical method' is extremely old and finds contemporary expression in Non-Realism - i.e. in not treating statements in theology or scripture as if they were historically 'real' events.

DEPTH PSYCHOLOGY is a branch of psychology concerned with the relationships between the conscious and the unconscious mind. It explores and tries to make meaning of the depths of the human mind, illuminating motive and gesture, searching for the origins of the attitudes we adopt towards ourselves and our world. The study of psychodynamics.

THE DEVIL is the archetypal spirit of division in the psyche.

EGO is the centre of consciousness; the awareness of myself as an I. Sometimes the word means pure, non-reflective consciousness, the very fine point of awareness, which is the bottom line, the undisputable basis of one's existence; but sometimes the term is used to refer to consciousness as an identifiable system of values, atitudes, memories, feelings, etc., which I think of as 'myself'. Some psychologists keep this distinction alive by speaking of an Ego as a point of awareness or pure consciousness and the Ego System as the sense of 'me'.

ESCHATOLOGY is the study of 'last things' - the end of the world; the coming of the 'Messiah'; the final Purposes of Life.

EROS is one of the Greek words for love. It was creative, sensual, passionate love; the force behind the attraction of lovers, but also behind the creative power of artists, of gardeners say, or the feelings of a mother for her child. Freud chose it to name the life-giving, creative and healing agent in the psyche - the self-regulative or integrative factors within the psyche - which the contemplatives called the Holy Spirit.

EVIL is life divided against itself; the sour corruptness arising out of the splitting off of areas of the psyche - the repression of unacceptable parts of the mind, such as anger or sexuality. The working out of the effects of alienation in the world.

EXISTENTIALISM is a kind of philosophy which gives priority to consciousness and conscious experience; whereas some philosophical systems give priority to the material world we know through our senses. To materialistic philosophies a gate post is real, but the imagination is not. According to existentialist thinkers we may exist in different categories of existence at the same time - as mother, lover, bus conductor, dreamer, etc. Any one kind of existence may be referred to as an EXISTENZ. Sometimes I may be unaware, unconscious, of particular existenz - my repressed grief or rage, for example; my early infancy; the way I exist to others and so on.

GNOSTICS - a name deriving from one of the Greek words for knowledge - the kind of knowledge which comes from intimate engagement with something. Christian Gnosticism was a religious movement coming into prominence in the second century AD. Gnosis represented the revealed knowledge of God.

GRACE is the process of healing. It is the gift of the Spirit or the product of co-operation between the Ego and its depths, arising spontaneously within the psyche and giving the person a sense of growing or changing.

HOLY SPIRIT - the active agent of the healing power of God, indwelling the soul. See EROS above.

HYPOSTATICAL UNION is the union of the soul with God; the integration of surface and depth; the spiritual marriage of the Ego and the Id.

HYSTERIA is from the Greek word for womb and was first used by Hippocrates to define the symptoms he recognised commonly in unfulfilled women. It has come to be used of symptoms which express, often symbolically, unconscious problems - such as anorexia, amnesia, vertigo or paralysis. Conditions where people are overwhelmed to the point of dramatically acting out feelings which cannot find direct forms of expression, because of a tyrannical super ego. The symptoms of hysteria occur, still, where unfulfilled aspects of men and women are struggling against our defences for freedom and truth.

ID is the name given by Freud to the Unconscious, especially to the organising centre of the unconscious. Das Id - meaning 'the It'.

INDIVIDUATION is the name given by Jung to the process of psychological maturation, of 'becoming a complete individual' in one's own right.

INTEGRATION has a similar meaning and refers to the coming together, the integrating of previously dissociated, split off parts of the mind.

JIVATMEN is the Hindu term for the surface self or Ego.

JOUISSANCE. There is no adequate English counterpart to this word. It means to enjoy or take pleasure - enjoyment of rights, also - it has sexual connotations (Jouir is slang for 'to come') - and also conveys a sense of joy.

KYRYGMA or KERYGMA is the name given to the proclamation of the standard, classical teaching of the early church.

LOGOS means literally 'Word'. It had a long use in philosophy before the time of Jesus and was used to refer to the 'Word' as the 'breathed out plan of God' - Spirit in action; the incarnation of Wisdom; the deepest intention of the psyche's Core. In John's Gospel the term was applied to Jesus as the Christ. The Christ was the Logos - our psychobiological potentiality, indwelling us as the oak indwells the acorn. Jesus was one who realised this potentiality.

MEDITATION originally meant a kind of meditative prayer, a half way house between discursive, spoken prayer and contemplatve prayer. But often it is used now to mean contemplative prayer as well.

METANOIA is a Greek word, used in the New Testament, where it is usually translated 'repentance'. It meant to change the mind or even to turn the mind upside down - a radical shift in the balance of the mind, in its values and intentions, its perception of itself and the world.

MYTH is a kind of universal dream; a narrative handed down generation by generation which contains spiritual or allegorical truth, psychological truth, about human nature.

NIRVANA - the cessation of desire; reaching union with our own depths; losing the delusions of Time and Separateness; literally to snuff out, as with a candle's flame. To be completely still.

OEDIPAL derives from Oedipus the hero of the Greek myth, which Sophocles made into a play. It represents the universal experience of abandonment and the tragic inter-relations of the parent-child triangle of mother, father and child. The name was given to the OEDIPAL POSITION, the stage between about two and a half and five years old, when this triangle is being shaped and the Ego Ideal (the notion of who I should be and how I should behave) being established. OEDIPAL EXPECTATIONS refers to the hope of affirmation, of winning over the parent of the opposite sex if I adhere to the Ego Ideal and the OEDIPAL SANCTIONS refers to the fears (perhaps of castration, but primarily of abandonment) if I do not live up to that Ideal - it is one root basis of the super ego and of conscience.

ONTOLOGY - the study of the nature of being, of existence, and of origins - first causes and the riddle of the move from infinity into the finite, from the atemporal to the temporal, from non-existence to existence.

OTHER may refer to God as the Other, or everything that is Other than me in the outside world or in the interior world of the mind. Other with a low case 'o' - other - may refer to a particular person or object.

PARAMATMEN is the name given in Hinduism to the deep centre of the psyche, the indwelling God, the deep Self.

PARANOID SCHIZOID POSITION was the name given by Melanie Klein to the developmental phase of our lives between four and eighteen months of age. She believed that bad handling at this stage was most important in the development of later pathology. Our sense of self was 'split' at this stage and we developed paranoid feelings of persecution, which remained with us unmodified unless future experience corrected them.

PERSONA comes from the Greek for an acting mask. It is the surface self I have cultivated and present to the world.

POSTMODERNISM is the name given to philosophical systems which attempt to retain the mystery of existence and which are suspicious of the modernist attempt to categorise and structure our thinking and knowledge, especially the use of hierarchical complements such as Right and Wrong; Male and Female; God and the Devil. Postmodernists believe our ways of thinking are so much determined by our language that we need to be constantly alert to our use of language and self-critical about our conceptions as we express them in language. They require a certain fluidity about our thinking, which is the opposite of dogmatism or the desire for certainty.

PRIMAL SCREAM is a term used by Janov to refer to the deep, primary pain of our first separation in weaning; the point where I split into acceptable and unacceptable parts. The movement from primary to secondary narcissism; the sense of being an undivided whole, containing everything within myself, and the sense of being a separate individual in the world, learned, it is sometimes said, by seeing myself reflected in the eyes of my mother.

PRIMARY AND SECONDARY THOUGHT PROCESSES: primary thought processes are those of the unconscious, expressing themselves, for example, in the symbolic, allegorical language of our dreams. The secondary thought processes are those of consciousness, using the language we learn from our culture.

REGRESSION is the process of returning to infantile or childhood ways of being; reliving early dramas, returning to lost feelings; feeling as we did when we were children.

SCHIZOIDAL POSITION is the name given to the stage of human mental development prior to the OEDIPAL position and includes the period of weaning. Regression to this stage of our development introduces us to the most intense feelings of hopelessness and helplessness, of not being able to cope, of abandonment. It is the stage in which the basic split between thoughts and feelings begins.

SCREEN MEMORIES are memories we remember from childhood as being especially significant in our development. Sometimes we remember them clearly and sometimes we have an amnesia for them. They may be recalled during session in therapy, or in a dream or some kind of abreactive experience, when they come vividly and directly into consciousness.

SELF AND self - a distinction between Self and self is made, especially in Jungian writings, to indicate the relationship between the 'self' as centre of consciousness and the 'Self' as centre of the Unconscious, or centre of the total psyche. Systems of contemplative prayer, such as yoga, were designed to bring about a union between these two centres of the mind.

SIN means a condition of error, a state of estrangement or separation from the Ground of Being, a disordered condition of the psyche; the experience of spiritual Exile.

SUPER-EGO is the name given to the conditioning influences of parents, extended family, peers and media as they are internalised and, as it were, superimposed on the Ego.

TRANSACTIONAL PARADIGM is the psychodynamic model of Parent, Child and Adult, taken out of the context of a form of psychotherapy known as Transactional Analysis

TRANSFERENCE AND COUNTER-TRANSFERENCE: transference is the transferring or projecting onto the therapist or other significant people in one's life feelings and expectations that derive from our handling as children. We transfer what we felt towards our parents and siblings. Counter-transference is what the therapist or other significant person feels in response to our transference - usually referring to what the therapist feels in response to the client's transference. It is what the therapist, in turn, brings into the session from her childhood relationships.

TRINITY - used by some theologians, Augustine e.g., as a psychodynamic model, representing God as the Ground of Being, from which we emerge; the Christ as the potentiality archetypally present in the Christ or God-image at the base of the soul; and the Holy Spirit as the active, creative, healing agent in the psyche, flowing from that archetypal image.

UNCONSCIOUS - the 'Unknown' part of the mind; the depths within us. Jung said the mind was like an iceberg - a small portion was above the surface, called the Conscious (known) mind and the larger portion, the Unconscious, was beneath the surface.

UNIVERSALISM - the belief that the Love of God is so irrestistible that all souls will be drawn to God and saved by God. Universal salvation - an idea often linked with Pluralism, the teaching that the essential truths of religious teaching are found in common within all the great religions of the world.

YOGA - meaning to unite. A bringing together of the two poles of the psyche - the jivatmen and the paramatmenn rooted in Brahman, the Ground of Existence.
128